A THEOLOGY OF HUMAN HOPE

A THEOLOGY

OF

HUMAN HOPE

RUBEM A. ALVES

CORPUS BOOKS: New York / Cleveland

CORPUS PUBLICATIONS

EDITORIAL OFFICES: *110 East 59th St., New York, N.Y. 10022*

SALES & DISTRIBUTION: *2231 West 110th Street, Cleveland, Ohio 44102*

Copyright © 1969 by Rubem A. Alves

Design by La Liberté & Rayner

LIBRARY OF CONGRESS CATALOG CARD NUMBER: 76-82271

Second Printing, February 1971

PRINTED IN THE UNITED STATES OF AMERICA

CONTENTS

FOREWORD

Beware, all ideologists, theologians, and theorists of the affluent, so-called "developed" world! The "Third World" of enforced poverty, hunger, powerlessness, and growing rage has found a ringing theological voice. Rubem Alves, a Brazilian Protestant and a brilliant, angry Latin American intellectual, speaks with an authority we cannot avoid noticing, not just in discussions about development and revolution, but wherever we assess the place of Christian faith in our convulsive contemporary world. With the appearance of this book, it is no longer possible for us to talk *about* the Third World theologically (if indeed it ever was). It is now clear that first of all we must listen. After that any further discussion must be *with*, not about. In Alves's own words, the Third World is neither mute nor reflexive. It will no longer allow either its political destiny or its theological self-definition to come from somewhere else.

Of course this will be a difficult adjustment for some of us to make, especially coming as it does so quickly on the heels of the black power upsurge. And there are similarities. With the rise of black power, the days were gone forever when we could erect theologies of interracial relations and issue pious calls for integration. We witnessed in our midst the appearance of a vigorous, confident movement of black Americans fully capable of speaking for themselves. Distressed but still eager to lend a helping hand somewhere, many of the high-purposed people who now felt excluded from the black struggle turned anxiously to the external proletariat of the Third World. Certainly, they hoped, if black people were no longer grateful clients for benevolent assistance, new wards could be found in the teeming *favellas* of Brazil, the rubber forests of Africa, or the rice paddies of Southeast Asia. Those who still felt the need of a white man's burden to bear looked to the Third World to find fresh recipients for the largess of the alliance for religious and social progress.

Now that possibility is gone too. Rubem Alves is not alone. There are other articulate theological writers in Latin America. In this book, however, these voices achieve a level of sophistication and refinement which will make it forever impossible to think of the Third World as theologically underdeveloped. Alves accomplished this feat by utilizing some of the affluent world's best thought, including the sociology of knowledge of Karl Mannheim, the scientific history of Thomas Kuhn, and even the philosophy of John Dewey. He blends these together to forge a genuinely radical theology, a theology of conflict, struggle, and hope. It is the theological equivalent of the guerilla using the captured weapons of the imperialist against him.

Using Mannheim, Alves shows just how much all contemporary theology is marooned in a morass of defensive ideology. Using Kuhn, he shows how much our willingness as theologians to quibble about the details of our systems further entraps us in obsolete paradigms that prevent conceptual breakthroughs. Alves combines the passionate and committed heart of the Third World with an intelligence honed and refined both by his political involvement and by his exposure to the salient ideas of the contemporary intellectual scene. His is the kind of mind that can bring into a single coherent focus the insights of Frantz Fanon, Karl Marx, Jürgen Moltmann, Mario Savio, Karl Barth, and Paul Lehmann and enrich them with the ideas of such Latin American intellectuals as Esdras Borges Costra and Paulo Friere. Instead of a mishmash, however, the result is a unified collage, a single sharp intellectually tensile weapon.

I have referred to Alves's thought in terms of a "weapon" for very good reasons. Even more important than the particular ideas Alves fuses is the singular way he puts them together. From his perspective, ideas are not isolated, nor are they segments to be fitted into an elegant and symmetrical system. For Alves, ideas live and breathe; they have their being in the struggle for human liberation itself. They are weapons whose truth is discovered only as they are used in combat.

There are, of course, some dangers involved in making any use of the weapons of the oppressor. Sometimes they explode in your hands. Sometimes they turn out to be the wrong gauge for your ammunition. This difficulty occasionally plagues Alves, but even on those rare occasions when the weapons fail, it is still a valuable experience for writer and reader alike. We can sometimes detect the weaknesses of our own intellectual armory when we see how inadequate it proves to be, even in expert hands, in a more demanding setting.

Sometimes the weapon-ideas of the oppressors turn out to be somewhat obsolescent. I think this also becomes clear in some of Alves's attempt to use them. This, however, is a judgment on which each reader will have to form his own opinion. For example, does Alves hew more closely than necessary to the theological tradition that emerged from the revival of biblical studies and the work of Karl Barth, Dietrich Bonhoeffer, and Paul Lehmann? What would he say to those young Christians who are simply not touched by biblical theology, that new generation of radical mystics, visionaries, and ecstatics who are certainly his allies in the struggle? Also, Alves could perhaps afford to be a little more "ecumenical" in the best sense of utilizing more resources outside the Protestant tradition. He alludes occasionally to Teilhard de Chardin and Leslie Dewart, but could his pulsing revolutionary theology receive enrichment, especially in the Latin American pressure cooker, from the insights of other modern Catholic thinkers?

Toward the end of this book he expresses, very rightly, some potent reservations about the traditional mainline Protestant doctrine of grace, at least in the way it has worked itself out. Might the creativity theology of Nicolas Berdyaev have added a larger dimension? Alves has made the best possible use of the more or less "neo-orthodox" arsenal he has taken over from his contemporary theological training. If these ideas sometimes misfire in his hands, it is a sign of the inadequacy of the ideas, not of the writer.

In any case, the alert reader of this book will recognize that in Alves he is encountering a restless, searching, and almost omnivorous mind. He is a man who can find his way through any system of ideas, using what seems helpful in the struggle for human liberation, discarding what is abstract, sterile, pompous, trivial. We can be confident that Alves will eventually incorporate into his thinking ideas quite outside the neo-reformation tradition. He is surely not the kind of man to be bound by the prejudices of his teachers.

Readers of this book will inevitably be struck by the similarity between its title and that of Jürgen Moltmann's well-known work, *A Theology of Hope.* Is there any kinship? Obviously Alves is significantly influenced by Moltmann and the so-called "theology of hope" movement. He sees God as the power that reaches toward man from an open future, making possible in history a new tomorrow. But for Alves, the name of God is not a cipher for some extrahistorical entity; it is faith's way of speaking about what is required to make and keep life human. Hope grows out of historical experience, especially the experience of liberation that occurs where there was no evidence that it could. Hope does not create pregnancy, says Alves, arguing against what he takes to be Moltmann's emphasis, rather pregnancy creates hope. God is present in the historical now, opening the way for a real future but grasped only in the struggle to make such a future.

How does Alves's thought relate to the so-called "radical theology" movement? In Alves's own mind, this question answers itself. He wants to encourage a theology that is radical in its political thrust and human consequences, not just in its rhetoric. He believes that the "death of God" theologians are talking about the demise of a deity who is still defined by classical ontological categories, and that they are therefore not very radical at all in the final analysis. They are quibbling about details but accepting the frame of reference. For Alves, on the other hand, transcendence must be found in the historical-political reality itself. Therefore it is the whole inherited paradigm of Western theological thinking that must undergo a death and rebirth. But its trauma must come, he insists, not just in thought but in praxis, in politics and in the struggle of the powerless to become the authors of history rather than its footnotes.

Speaking of footnotes, it may seem to some readers that Alves has somewhat overdone the quaint academic custom of argument by citation. They should remember, however, that this book was originally written as a doctoral dissertation and therefore it presumably had to conform to the bizarre practices that still cramp and harass graduate study in religion, or any other field, for that matter. The fact that Alves was able to distill such a cogent book from such an unlikely enterprise says much for his persistence and originality. Also, as this particular reader discovered, it is not really necessary to check the notes section every time one encounters a footnote. The general reader will get even more from the book if he glances through the note page of a given chapter before he reads the chapter itself, and then checks back again only if his curiosity about a particular reference becomes unbearable. The argument of the book stands on its own feet.

A Theology of Human Hope draws together, in style and in content, many of the loose threads that have been dangling in the ether since the recent frazzling out of the theological consensus. In his torrential piling on of words and metaphors Alves often reminds one of the angry early Barth. In his fascination with language he is reminiscent of the language philosophers and theologians—with one very important difference: Alves is more concerned with the cultural and political setting out of which language emerges than he is with its grammar. For those interested in the much-touted Christian-Marxist dialogue itself, he is in fact a personification of its best fruits. Both in his critical use of some Marxist categories, and in his realization that theology must be a theory of *praxis*, he demonstrates what the dialogue can contribute to theology.

Finally I would like to add a word about Alves's relation to my own theological work. A few years back I wrote a small book entitled *God's Revolution and Man's Responsibility* (Valley Forge: Judson Press, 1965), in which I tried to probe some of the same themes Alves explores, especially the relationship between God's initiative and man's creativity in history. At that time I was working with some of the same theological resources Alves uses, especially Bonhoeffer. In this book Alves exceeds all the hopes I had for that book and resolves with immeasurably more profundity and scholarship the problems I discussed. I am not as satisfied with his discussion of *The Secular City* in this book, especially his placing me among the fans of "technologism." From my own perspective, the most important chapters in *The Secular City* were the ones in which I tried to fashion a theology of social change. Still there are some points at which Alves's criticism is accurate, luckily mostly on notions about which I have subsequently changed my mind, partly under the pressure of more politically revolutionary thinkers like him. I am grateful to him for carrying further some of the impulses I touched on in those two books and for doing so with such competence and zest.

What interests me even more, however, is the similarity between the concluding chapter of *A Theology of Human Hope* and the themes I have developed in *The Feast of Fools* (Cambridge: Harvard University Press, 1969).

Alves concludes this book first with a plea for the indispensable role of imagination in politics and then bears down on some of today's revolutionaries. He calls for a new fusion of Apollonian and Dionysian elements, a glad celebration of the body, a joyous combination of eros with agape in the battle to liberate man from both oppression and repression. The book could not end on a more welcome or needed note. I am persuaded that those dedicated to the battle for fundamental social change need not be joyless ascetics and that those who find delectation in the tastes and smells of the present need not become fat and placid. Alves has added to our effort to forge a theology of revolution something that perhaps only a Latin American could, a large helping of sheer human felicity. His revolutionary theology is written to be played not only *vivace* but *con brio*. Alves is not satisfied merely to talk about human hope, he sparks and nourishes it.

HARVEY COX

Roxbury, Massachusetts
20 July 1969

PREFACE

The reflections that the reader will find in the following pages should not be understood as a new idea or hypothesis created and advanced by the author. I do not intend them to be so. My purpose is much more modest. I simply try to explore critically the elements and possibilities of a new language that some groups of Christians are attempting to learn.

This language is being created in a historical situation. The starting point and locus of my reflections are, accordingly, radically historical. I cannot, therefore, justify *in abstracto* or *a priori* the reflections I offer, because they are born out of a situation that cannot be explained on these grounds. My theological explorations are thus intended to be nothing more than an expression of participation in a community of Christians who are struggling to discover how to speak faithfully the language of faith in the context of their commitment to the historical liberation of man.

Since these reflections arise out of my relative and provisional historical situation, they share the same provisional and relative character. They must, therefore, remain unfinished and open. Someone in a different historical situation could make a different choice. I cannot say that my historical experience is truer than his. There is always the element of personal choice and commitment, the risk of faith involved.

It is obvious that historical commitment has a decisive import upon interpretation. It is from the perspective of the present moment that I try to make sense of what is going on. It is from this same present that I read my past. It is this commitment to the present that provides the center from which the horizons of the present merge with the horizons of the past, thereby providing the context for the exploration of the horizons of the future. From a different perspective the same biblical material could probably be read in a different way. Exegesis is always done from one's relative position in history. We could ask, with Kierkegaard: Where is it that we are outside our own existence? Where is it that we can think *sub specie aeternitatis?* There is no such place.

I therefore start from what is going on now amid certain Christian communities. But my point of departure is also my destination. It is for the sake of what is going on that these reflections are undertaken. They are reflections en route, a simple footnote at the service of the on-going adventure of creating a new tomorrow.

ACKNOWLEDGMENTS

I want to express my deep gratitude to the administration and faculty of Princeton Theological Seminary both for the opportunity to study and for the funds that were made available for the completion of my academic work; to Drs. C. C. West, Diogenes Allen, and M. Richard Shaull, whose critique helped me immensely in organizing and clarifying my thought; and to Dr. Robert Evans, who kindly corrected the manuscript written by one whose mother tongue is not English.

I have a special word of gratitude to Dr. Richard Shaull, a close friend for more than fifteen years, whose thought and words have always been the expression of his permanent personal and intellectual commitment to the creation of a new future for man.

A THEOLOGY OF HUMAN HOPE

CHAPTER ONE

IN SEARCH OF FREEDOM

Man is a historical being. He is not born in the world of things, persons, and time as a finished product. His being is not prior to history. He becomes what he is through the history of his relations with his environment. He is not, therefore, simply a being *in* the world; he comes into being *with* the world. Man and world do not come together as two alien entities that happen to be in a relation of contact, as a mind or ego that simply takes notice of that which stands over against them, that is, matter. If this were so, man would be able to perceive the world; he would be able to take snapshots of it, as a camera does. But man and the world would remain permanently alien to one another. Man would not be able to be receptive to the world. He would not be able to be penetrated, transformed, created by it. And the world, equally, would not be made more human. Man could know and handle this world, but it could not bear the stamp of the human.

Man changes because he is not a monad. He is open. Because he is open, he is able to respond instead of simply react. To react is within the sphere of the biological. To respond, however, belongs to the sphere of freedom. Man responds because he discovers his world as a message which is addressed to him, as a horizon into which he can project himself. And when he responds the world becomes different. It becomes historical. It ceases to be the isolated sphere of nature and bears now the stamp of freedom. And precisely in this same act man becomes historical because he becomes different. Man, after his response, is not the same as he was before.

In the sphere of history both man and the world remain open-ended because the possibilities of the relations between them are never exhausted.

Man's language is a mirror of his historicity. It not only emerges out of the metabolism which goes on between him and his world but is uttered as a response to the concrete situations in which he finds himself. It is obvious that language is not always the expression of man's historicity. Very often it is just a set of symbols which function as a shorthand way of picturing the behavior of nature, or which simply describe what has objectively happened. Just as a film, after it is processed, reproduces in a different dimension the objective world of things, so language can function as the processed result of man's snapshots of the world. When language is historical, however, it tells man's story. It does not simply describe. It contains *man's interpretation* of the message and challenge that his world addresses to him and expresses *man's response* to this message and challenge. It tells from within, through his eyes, how he understands himself in this world, what he believes to be his vocation, place, possibilities, direction, and function in his world.

Historical language cannot be stabilized. It remains as open-ended as man's consciousness and history. It cannot, therefore, be reduced to a set of mathematical or ahistorical symbols. As man rediscovers and recreates himself, thereby redefining his self-understanding and vocation, so language changes. It remains moving as man moves. This becomes very clear when we compare the language of adolescence with the language of adulthood. The adolescent's language is like a river, fluid, plastic, in an endless process of creating new words and abandoning old ones. Its ephemeral character indicates the rhythm of the adolescent's experience, the violent process of change, the effort to become free from old values, the search for new meanings, the absence of fixation on past gains. It is a language that represents a search. The language of adults, on the contrary, tends to be the language of those who have become stabilized, if not emotionally, at least as part of the society in which they live, and whose language they have adopted. This language indicates therefore a different type of experience, which can hardly be defined as a search.

To the extent that language expresses and defines a certain experience, it determines the limits of a community. A community depends on the sense of a common experience, a similar self-understanding, a shared direction, for its existence as community. When men speak a common language, they thereby recognize themselves as participating in a common understanding of the world, as committed to a similar project, as united by a common vocation toward it. But as it creates community, language separates man and man. "For language," remarks Ebeling, "which makes understanding possible for one man, prevents understanding for another. Language creates simultaneously understanding and incomprehension, it binds and it separates."[1] It expresses the tension that exists between a community that has taken a certain decision as to its vocation in the world and all the other communities that are either indifferent or opposed to its "ultimate concern."

The appearance of a new language announces, therefore, the coming into being of a new experience, a new self-understanding, a new vocation, and consequently, a different man and community, a new subject. Through its language, expressive of its unique self-consciousness, the new community singles itself out from the old. New words are then created and new meanings are given to old words. Through his language this new subject makes himself present in history. To engage in dialogue with this man, to respond to the new reality that he represents, is thus an occasion for changes in the one who responds. One cannot respond without becoming different. If one does not become different it is because one has become crystallized and frozen and has ceased to be historical.

A Consciousness in Search of Freedom: Political Humanism

Today we are contemplating the emergence of a new type of consciousness and are hearing the new language that it speaks. As we indicated before, a new language, since it expresses a certain type of experience, determines a community. This new consciousness and new language, therefore, announce the birth of a new community. We will refer to it, tentatively, as the "world proletariat." It will become obvious that the word "community" is not totally adequate to describe the world proletariat. In spite of this we will use it to indicate that, although there is a tremendous variety of elements separating those who speak the new language, the fact remains that they are united by a common understanding of their historical experience and therefore by a similar structure of consciousness.

It is of utmost importance to keep in mind that the subject of our exploration is not the world in which this consciousness finds itself but rather the way this consciousness understands itself in the world. "Proletariat" will therefore not be used primarily as descriptive of objective social, economic, or political relations and structures, but rather as descriptive of a consciousness which understands itself as proletarian in the world in which it finds itself. We will be concerned with the description of this consciousness and not with a scientific exploration and critique of its claims. Moreover, we are neither suggesting that the deprived person always has a proletarian consciousness, or that this consciousness can emerge only from the proletariat. It can be found, on the one hand, among many student groups in nations that economically and socially belong to the affluent parts of our world; and, on the other hand, it has not appeared among many of those who economically and socially belong to the "have-not" groups. When we refer to the world proletariat we thus have in mind a new consciousness, a new self-understanding, which speaks a new language and has a specific sense of vocation. But more than that: when we speak about the world proletariat we are thereby indicating that this new consciousness has become a truly ecumenical phenomenon, which unites peoples from the Third World with blacks, students, and other groups of the affluent nations. This consciousness, therefore, is not delimited by national, economic, social, or racial boundaries.

The first association which the expression world proletariat brings to our mind is poverty. We think about the masses of workers who lived in the most outrageous conditions in the countries which first went through the industrial revolution. This is a good point to start with, because it seems that this consciousness first came into being among those who discovered this basic fact of their lives: their poverty. It was the acknowledgment of this fact which led many poor nations to call themselves the "Third World." The expression "Third World" is a refusal to be boxed into the ideological classification which the cold war created. They did not belong to either of the two worlds—East or West. Theirs was a Third World, the world of poverty, the world of the have-nots. They were underdeveloped. At first it was thought that this situation was simply before development, on its way toward development. Their hope was that they would eventually reach the so-called take-off point, the point at which their inertia would be overcome and with it a qualitative change would occur: they would move to the other side and would be part of the world of rich nations. These hopes, however, are disappearing. The proletarian consciousness became aware of the brutal reality of the growing gap between the rich and the poor nations. The rich get richer. The poor become poorer. The underdeveloped nations could not avoid a sense of failure or even of abnormality, because of their inability to provide even what was barely essential for the physical survival of their peoples, as they daily face the reality of famine and starvation. At the same time they are confronted with the economies of abundance, waste, and warfare of the wealthy nations of the world.

The experience of the black man in the United States is basically the same. What was he? Nothing more than a man who lived beyond the border of an economy of abundance. The fruits of that economy were there before him: the fine schools, suburbia, the good jobs, the expensive cars, the life of leisure. But the Negro was not allowed into this exclusive world. There he remained, on the margin of this society, living in the "holes" which had been left by the white man. His was the society of the ghetto, of the slum, in shocking contrast to the white society of suburbia. As the man of the Third World dreamt about becoming a part of the developed nations, the black man dreamed about integration, about becoming accepted by and in the white society. He wanted to have a part in it, to live in the same neighborhoods, to go to the same restaurants, to have the same jobs, to attend the same schools and churches as the whites did. He wanted to be liberated from racial segregation in order to be allowed into the world of economic well being.

However, a remarkable change occurred in the black man's understanding of himself. Both the man in the Third World and the black man in the United States of America became aware that although poverty was terribly painful, that was not the most basic of their problems. They came to realize that they were not simply poor. *They were made poor.* Their poverty was the consequence of a colonial relationship in which the powerful dominated and controlled the lives of the weak. Colonialism was not just a situation of the past. It was intrinsic to the relations between poor and rich and indeed the cause of the poverty of the poor. But more than that, colonialism came to be seen as a relationship in which those who are dominated are not allowed to become the creators of their own history. They are reduced to a situation of reflexiveness. This means that the lives of the colonial nations or groups were not planned according to their own needs, but according to the needs of the economy of the dominant groups. The lives of the dominated became then sub-systems which always reacted according to the stimuli of the masters, without ever being able to change the relationships of domination under which they were. Underdevelopment accordingly began to be understood not in temporal but in relational terms, as *under*-development, as the result of a relationship whereby the powerful and affluent dominated the weak and poor. For the proletarian consciousness this explained why, after all the programs of aid for development sponsored by the developed nations, the underdeveloped nations became a prey, as never before, to the abnormal growth of their internal contradictions, to the deterioration of their economies, and to the widening gap which separated them from the rich nations. How could it be otherwise if they were not allowed to be the subjects of their own development?

The North American blacks had a similar experience. Their past was the history of their impotence under the domination of the white man. They could not remember when they had been the subjects of their own history. The only thing that their memory contained was the presence of the anonymous "they" of the white society which forced them to the situation of reflexiveness. As far as they could remember, their future had been imposed and not freely chosen. They had never been the creators of their own history but rather the object of someone else's history.

The proletarian consciousness then moved from consciousness of poverty to consciousness of impotence or of having been made impotent before history. It is this feeling which makes it possible for a new generation of students to become identified with the cause of the black man and with that of the nations of the Third World. Obviously they are not united in their poverty. These students are well fed, well dressed, and have all the doors of affluence open to them. They are united in a common experience of not being allowed to be the creators of their own history. They are put in a university which, in the words of Clark Kerr, is "a factory for the production of knowledge and technicians to service society's many bureaucracies." If this is a normal thing for those who now control society, for the students it means that they are being prepared to fit in and to serve the *given* system. They have thus to learn how to be "in a game in which all the rules have been made up, and which one cannot really amend." For the sake of the given system and as a prior condition for being admitted into it "they must suppress the most creative impulses that they have."[2]

Consequently students came to see themselves as victims of an adult conspiracy that creates educational institutions which are really "factories" which "turn out people with all the sharp edges off, the well-rounded person."[3] They consider themselves, therefore, as an exploited class, since their labor is not to be used for the building of *their* world but rather for the preservation of the adult's world. "The adults are suspicious of their youth, and are particularly afraid of the directions which this same youth could imprint upon the future which is still the adult's future," comments Pierre Furter. The adult rationlizes: "The youth is good . . . but must be oriented." However, "the goal of this cynical and hypocritical attitude is not 'to make the youth the cause of history,' but rather to make them its object. One has, then, to invent techniques which will condition, influence, orient—and why not?—brainwash them. All this in order that the youth do that which we—the adults— believe that they must do."[4]

Here is the common denominator that identifies the

proletarian consciousness: the consciousness of being dominated by a power which does not allow it to create its own history. Within these relationships of domination "history has in fact come to an end."[5]

Colonialism is not a new situation. It iş indeed very old. What is new is that now the consciousness that was before submerged into and conditioned by this relationship has emerged from it. In the past, colonialism was so successful that it was able not only to maintain an oppressed man but an oppressed consciousness as well. An oppressed consciousness is that which is domesticated by the situation of oppression in which it finds itself. It is a consciousness which really became reflexive, unable to be subject, deprived of a sense of direction and of historical vocation. Dominated by reflexiveness, this consciousness could not speak. Unable to enter in critical dialogue with their environment, as a consequence of the relationship of domination which oppressed them, these societies became "mute."[6]

Their language was not an expression of a historical self-consciousness, since they had been reduced to ahistoricity by colonialism. They spoke a language that did not belong to themselves: they repeated, like an echo, the slogans of those who dominated them.[7]

Determined by reflexiveness and mutism, the oppressed consciousness was reduced to paralysis. Creative action is possible only in the context of hope and power, when man envisages a future and finds himself powerful enough to master his environment, through his action, in order to achieve his goal. The oppressed consciousness, however, is deprived of both these elements. It has no future. The future belongs to the master. Action, therefore, does not create a new future, because it is always determined for the master. The oppressed consciousness, therefore, is incapable of planning the future. It gambles about it. It takes chances. It retracts its action, defensively refusing to work. It cannot do otherwise. The oppressed man's inaction is the reflex of the impotence to which he was reduced by colonialism. His "laziness" (to which the master so often points in order to explain the poverty of the poor) is not a vice. It is rather the creation of the relationship of domination within which he is compressed and the natural and necessary defensive reaction against it.[8]

Today, however, something has changed. The man still oppressed is speaking a different language. It is a language of his own, which indicates that he has emerged into history. He sees the situation of oppression that dominates him. But his consciousness is no longer domesticated. He is determined to liberate himself historically. In the past, the future was closed for him and his consciousness was closed to the future. Today, although the future still remains closed, his consciousness is open for the future. He inserts himself into his historical present as a contradiction to it, as a negation which presses toward a new tomorrow. He has become a historical subject with a definite sense of vocation. The new language announces that a new man is born into history.

The contradiction between the openness of the consciousness for the creation of a new future and the reality of the closedness of the societies into which it is inserted gives to this new language a fundamentally negative character. The oppressive character of its present "is transformed within [it] into a stubborn refusal of the animal condition."[9] One does not have to agree with Frantz Fanon in order to understand the analysis he makes of the consciousness of oppressed people. Colonialism, he says, distorted them as human beings. It is a form of violence, because it robs man of any free relationship with his world and his future. The violence under which this man was became part of his own being. It created him in its own image. And now, as he decides to take his future and destiny into his own hands, he cannot avoid the explosion of that violence which colonialism injected into his veins. He becomes violent in order to be returned to the normality of a free man, by the destruction of the power which made him inhuman.[10] This violence is the expression of his refusal of the animal condition to which the masters reduced him.

This process can be described as the emergence of freedom. Man ceases to be a one-dimensional being, whose consciousness is submerged into the facts exterior to it. It gains distance. It looks at the facts as something against which it is opposed. Man no longer is a reflexive repetition of his contacts with the world. He is born to freedom as he becomes critical.[11]

This basic negation, therefore, is not born out of the slave's envy for the "things" of the masters. It does not envisage an inversion of the world whereby the affluent will be plundered by the envious masses which will then become rich. The central issue is not "things" but freedom to create history. This is why a society which creates and perpetuates man as a reflexive animal is rejected by this consciousness.

The transformation the Civil Rights movement has experienced seems to prove this point. At first, the Negroes were oppressed by the sense of their economic deprivation. They wanted to be integrated into the white society in order to have a share of its affluence. However, precisely when the white liberals were starting to move in order to make a place for the Negroes, the black man discovered that his fundamental problem was not economic deprivation, but rather his powerlessness. He was not the creator of his future. He discovered himself "as a unique case of colonialism" in the middle of a society of abundance. The black community was a "colony" and consequently the blacks had "their political decisions made for them by the colonial masters."[12] He was led then to realize that integration demanded "that the Negro foreswear his identity as a Negro,"[13] by becoming a part "of the mainstream institutions of the society from which he [had] been traditionally excluded."[14] The new consciousness, however, saw things differently. The main problem was not participation in the affluence of the white society. The black man is to recover himself by becoming the creator of his own history. But this is possible only if he has power. His consciousness swings then from integration to Black Power. He wants to play a creative role in history.[15]

The protest of students has the same significance. They are profoundly aware of the inhumanity of the white society. Its inhumanity does not lie in its inability to deliver goods; it does this with the utmost success. Students protest because they feel themselves to be an exploited group being prepared to function as a part of a society that takes itself for granted, that is closed and final, in spite of all the contradictions it is creating in terms of internal and international injustice. They refuse integration. "In increasing numbers they do not desire to become part of that society. From their peripheral social position they are able to maintain human values, values which they know will be distorted or destroyed when they enter the compromising, practical, 'adult world.' "[16] They feel that the white society must be rejected either by a radical retreat from it, by a style of life which negates the ideal image that this same society has created, or by radical action against it. "Rather die than be standardized, replaceable, and irrelevant."[17]

As the first expression of man's freedom, as it reacts against the suffering his situation creates, negation may seem to the detached observer as something irrational, devoid of clear purpose. And that is very often the case. How could it be otherwise? The detached man finds it easy to be cold, to act in terms of calculation. But how can one expect this from the man who experiences death in life? Is his reaction, his negation, less human, less true, less authentic, because of that? This man would probably be unable to define with the precision of scientific logic the grounds and goal of his negation. It emerges, at first, as "guts reality," as a shout of pain, anger, and refusal. But it expands; it becomes a "symphony of negation" which includes not only the type of violence described by Fanon, but the humor of the joker who ridicules the status quo and the determination of the scientist and philosopher to perform the role of critics of their societies (and not merely the analytical and descriptive functions commonly assigned to them).

The surprising fact about this critical consciousness that negates the world into which it is inserted is that it does not remain negative. To negate means to reject the ultimate validity of the present state of affairs. But because the present is not seen as final, it becomes possible and necessary to search for those possibilities that are absent from the present. The consciousness then projects itself in the direction of the future, giving birth to hope. "This climate of hope," remarks Paulo Freire, "is born at the exact moment when a given society begins to turn upon itself and finds out that it is not finished, that there is an infinite number of tasks to be accomplished. The hopelessness and pessimism which existed before about its present and future, as well as that naive optimism, give place to a critical optimism, to hope."[18] One discovers then that "history has not ended, that a better society is possible, and that it is worth dying for."[19]

This consciousness is thus, on the one hand, determined by its apprehension of the inhuman and therefore contradictory character of society, and on the other, by the discovery of both the unfinished character of the world and the open horizons that invite man's creativity and experimentation. Like a lover, however, it does not allow its passion to remain subjective. It wants to fertilize the earth, to bear a child, to create a new tomorrow in which its negation and hope will become historical. But this possibility is transformed into reality only through the mediation of free acts. "Only when the consciousness is aware of the fact that it is the cause of free acts," remarks A. V. Pinto, "can it become the origin of a just plan of existence for the community, that is to say, the plan of its freedom."[20] The new tomorrow, therefore, is not to be mediated by the logic immanent in the given facts of the present state of affairs. Indeed, it is this same logic which is being negated by the new subject. What he wants is to introduce into history a logic not derived from the given, but from the humanizing creation of freedom. It negates the divinity and finality of the logic of facts. The human, thus understood, does not emerge from the facts that are now creating the inhuman. The human is the creation of a human subject whose consciousness is set against the contradiction of the facts. Only this consciousness is able to shape the new tomorrow in accordance with its hope.

Freedom is thus subordinated to and put at the service of the concrete conditions of human life in the world. At the end of freedom one must find a "gift"—a more human world. Society will "be rational and free," remarks Marcuse, "to the extent to which it is organized, sustained, and reproduced by an essentially new subject,"[21] the subject which is not submerged in and determined by the logic of the given facts. Thus, a more human society, a more human world are mediated by an act whereby the freedom of the new subject becomes historical. Only through his act does man become the creator of history.

This man cannot, therefore, accept the masters' proposal to create his future for him. If his future is to be created by the masters, he will remain "object," and the new future will not be the embodiment of his negation and hope but rather another triumph of the master over him. Here is the danger of aid programs which the wealthy nations propose to the poor nations of the world as the solution for their underdeveloped situation.

> The great danger of welfare and aid programs is the violence of their anti-dialogal character which, by imposing mutism and passivity upon man, do not give him the necessary conditions for the unfolding or opening of his consciousness which, in authentic democracies, has to be increasingly critical. It is this lack of opportunity for decision and for man's participating responsibility . . . which leads the solutions proposed by aid programs to contradict man's vocation to be a subject.[22]

Humanization, therefore, is not created by economic panaceas. It exists to the extent to which man, as free subject, creates his future, the future which liberates him from the passivity under which the master keeps him. "Man is only truly man," observes Paul VI in *Populorum Progressio,* "in as far as master of his own acts and judge of their worth, he is author of his own advancement."[23]

The new self-consciousness of the black man and the student shares this same view, that from a closed and inhuman society no new tomorrow will emerge by itself. Free human beings have to take power in their own hands in order to create it. They know that "the masters are capable of improving the life of the slave and of improving his exploitation." But only "the slave is capable of abolishing the masters and of cooperating with them."[24]

In order to understand this new self-consciousness it is not enough to have in mind the dialectic between negation and hope that determines it. We must be aware of its radically historical and secular character. It is determined by negation and hope not because it takes as its point of departure a truth higher than history. It negates history in the name of history and from within history. The present is negated because man, in his insertion into its midst, apprehends what creates pain, suffering, injustice, and defuturization in history. Because the present is historically painful and therefore dehumanizing, it must be negated. On the contrary, hope is not derived from an ahistorical idea of the perfect society; it is rather simply the positive shape which the negation of the negative and inhuman of the present takes. The consciousness' "dissatisfaction does not come from its perception of a pattern prior to the

perception of the facts, and for this reason eternal," comments
A. V. Pinto, "but rather from its disagreement with the pattern of
the future, extracted from its perception of the present reality. The
plan is induced from reality, it is empirical, which is the basis for
its effectiveness."[25] This consciousness thus emerges from history
and remains turned towards history.

Man reaches here a new self-understanding. He discovers himself as a historical subject, as one who can create a new tomorrow.
This is his vocation and in it he finds his humanity.

The creation of history, however, is possible only through
power. Only through the historical exercise of power is the inhuman today negated and the way to a more human future made
open. It is because man is present in his act that the new day which
it creates can be more friendly. His use of power is, therefore, the
historical form which his freedom, his transcendence over the
given facts, takes. But the use of power is politics. This is why this
new consciousness believes that the new man and the new tomorrow are to be created in and through an activity which is political
in character. Politics would be the practice of freedom, the activity
of the free man for the creation of a new tomorrow. In this context
politics is no longer understood as the activity of the few, the play
of power among the elites. It is the vocation of man, because every
man is called to participate, in one way or another, in the creation
of the future. Politics thus becomes for this consciousness the new
gospel, the annunciation of the good news that, if man emerges
from passivity and reflexivity, as the subject of history, a new future
can be created. It challenges man: "Seek first the kingdom of
politics and his power, and all these things shall be yours."[26]

We have here a new understanding of man—indeed, a new
paradigm for humanization. Human liberation is the result of man's
responsible activity, as he takes the risk of creating a more friendly
tomorrow. If one asks this man: what is the shape of this new
tomorrow? What is the humanization you are driving at?—he will
probably speak about the exigencies of his situation, the tasks which
lie ahead of his society. But he will not have an a priori definition
of the human. Because in the process of creating the world, he
believes, man becomes different and discovers new dimensions and

criteria for humanity. Therefore the language about humanization can be spoken only "on the way," in the historical context in which man finds himself and from the concrete commitments which his today and his tomorrow require from him. It is a new type of humanism, not based on an abstract definition of the essence of man but rather on man's freedom to re-create his world and himself anew, according to his own choice. It is a political humanism. And it is more than that: it is a new type of messianism, which believes that man can be free by the powers of man alone: humanistic messianism.[27]

The Consciousness of Political Humanism and Its Critique of the Language of "Technologism"

The language of political humanism is a language of hope. It negates but it does not remain negative. It looks to the future and it loves the possibilities that could become historical if man accepted the challenge to become the creator of history.

The hope which it presents, however, is almost eclipsed by the bright promises of the language of "technologism," that is, a form of consciousness that regards technology as the way to the future, and which cites the wonders of technology as proof of its conviction. Here we find a language of an overwhelming optimism: it claims to have the power and to know how to transform the earth from a desert into a garden. Mark Twain expressed this infinite hope and expectation in a letter which he wrote to Walt Whitman for his seventieth birthday.

> You have lived just the seventy years which are greatest in the world's history and richest in benefit and advancement to its peoples. These seventy years have done much more to widen the interval between man and the other animals than was accomplished by any of the five centuries which preceded them. What great births you have witnessed! The steam press, the steamship, the steel ship, the railroad, the perfect cotton gin, the telegraph, the phonograph, photogravure, the electrotype, the gaslight, the electric light, the sewing machine, and the amazing, infinitely varied and innumerable products of

coal tar, those latest and strongest marvels of a marvelous age. And you have seen even greater births than these; for you have seen the application of anesthesia to surgery-practice, whereby the ancient dominion of pain, which began with the first created life, came to an end on this earth forever. . . . Yes, you have indeed seen much—but tarry for a while, for the greatest is yet to come. Wait thirty years, and *then* look out over the earth! You shall see marvels upon marvels added to those whose nativity you have witnessed; and conspicuous about them you shall see the formidable Result—man at almost his full stature at last!—and still growing, visibly growing while you look. . . . Wait till you see that great figure appear, and catch the far glint of the sun upon his banner; then you may depart satisfied, as knowing you have seen him for whom the earth was made, and that he will proclaim that human wheat is more than human tares, and proceed to organize human values on that basis. *(signed)* MARK TWAIN.[28]

This is the general tone of the language of the prophets of the cybercultural era. Within its sphere the tomorrow and hopes of man become the realities of today. It says to man: "Tell me what your dreams are and I will teach you how to transform them into reality. Tell me what are the problems of the world, what is it that makes you suffer, and I will show how to bring about liberation."

Mankind suffers because it does not have enough to eat. Technology knows how to produce food for the whole world. It proclaims that people no longer need to die of famine, because it has set mankind "on the threshold of a new era in human history, an era in which heretofore undreamed-of abundance can eliminate want and the necessity of competition for scarce resources."[29] "We can make enough to allow everyone to share in the goods of the earth,"[30] say its prophets.

Mankind suffers because of the apocalyptic threat of population explosion. Technology knows how to solve it. It is able to create wonder pills and contraceptive devices that will make it possible for every man to rationalize the size of his family, so that it will conform not only to his economic resources but also to his psychological, social, and spiritual needs.

Mankind suffers because labor has contributed to oppress and dehumanize man. Has not the accusation of communists, marxists, socialists, Christians, humanists, and all men concerned about justice been that the workers are exploited and that their pay does not correspond to the real value of their work? Has not the hard reality of daily life been that work, instead of being liberating, is rather an inhuman experience? Technology knows how to liberate man from this situation. Through cybernation, "the hitching of the computer to the machine" which "reduces the human role to programming the task and maintaining the equipment" man will be emancipated from work as a burden. How will this miracle be accomplished?

> . . . there will be fewer jobs [and] the jobs remaining will demand ever-higher level of skills; but [as the result] we shall be able for the first time to produce enough goods and services so that no person will need to live in poverty and deprivation.[31]

"We need no longer force people to work at what the market defines as important," comments R. Theobald; "we can set them free to do what they like. This is one result of providing everyone with an income—we can now afford to say that if you want to cultivate your garden, if you want to improve the face of our cities, if you want to work with the culturally deprived, we will pay you to do this."[32] We are thus living in an "era in which vast quantities of free time will be available to those who want it."[33]

> This would mean that people who wanted to work at marketable jobs would do so and those whose interests and talents are not salable, such as poets and painters, would be able to live without prostituting their gifts. . . . The traditional division between work and play, or labor and leisure, would be broken down.[34]

The most stupendous result of this revolution, however, would be the birth of a new man, free from worries about material needs and therefore free for a new spiritual dimension.

> A psychology of abundance produces initiative, faith in life, solidarity. The fact is that most men are still geared psychologically to the economic facts of scarcity, when the industrial world is in the process of entering a new era of economic abundance. . . . A further effect of the guaranteed income . . . would be that the spiritual and religious problems of human existence would become real and imperative. Until now man has been occupied with work (or has been too tired after work)

to be too seriously concerned with such problems as "What is the meaning of life?" "What do I believe in?" "What are my values" "Who am I?" etc. If he ceases to be mainly occupied by work, he will either be free to confront these problems seriously, or he will become half mad from direct or compensated boredom. From all this it would follow that economic abundance, liberation from fear of starvation, would mark the transition from the pre-human to a truly human society.[35]

Van Leeuwen's *Christianity in World History* adds a theological note to the hope that technology brings.[36] His thesis is that technology, through its power to break open closed societies, is able to liberate history from the idols which bring it to a halt. It thereby thrusts man into new dimensions of freedom and experimentation. Technology would be thus the deadly enemy of stability and the mother of revolution. This thesis is not new—Marx had a similar view. He believed that technology would be the mother of the revolutionary class, the proletariat. What is radically new in van Leeuwen's book is that he claims that technology is a child and expression of the historicizing impetus of the biblical faith and its permanent conflict with the closed, final, sacred, ontocratic societies. Technology is a unique phenomenon in a civilization that was formed under the influence of "discernible spiritual motives," such as "a particular view of God, man, and the world."[37] These spiritual motives performed a desacralizing and secularizing function in relation to the world and nature, thereby giving to man the freedom to know and to dominate them. One can therefore affirm on historical grounds, van Leeuwen believes, that the "technological revolution was [not only] nurtured in the bosom of Christian civilization but [is] indeed one of its 'children.' "[38] The secularizing thrust of the struggle between the biblical God and the powers of stability achieves in Western civilization its greatest victory because now, for the first time "in the history of mankind . . . the ontocratic pattern has been broken through and superseded by the technological pattern."[39]

The historicizing power of technology, however, is contagious. When the Western powers invaded the non-Western civilizations and enslaved them under a colonial relationship, they brought their technology along, as one of the instruments for exploitation. The introduction of technology, however, was like the injection of a revolutionary virus. It broke the old societal patterns, thereby liberating the colonial peoples, in the very act of their exploitation, from their provincialism and self-enclosed world. This is not intended to be a justification of colonialism but simply the description of what historically happened. Once the old patterns were broken these peoples found themselves living within history, within a context where the status quo has no ultimacy and a new and different tomorrow must be sought. It was this secularizing thrust of technology that gave birth to the movements of liberation of the second half of the twentieth century as the unpremeditated and unwelcomed upshot of Western technology, which was intended to be nothing more than a more efficient method of exploitation and domination.

This process, however, is not simply one in which open societies are being created. As societies are liberated from vertical absolutes and spheric limits for experimental and open horizons, a new man comes into being, the man who finds his home in the secular and provisional world, the man who can dispense with the temple and with all forms of religious or metaphysical absolutes. He is free for history as a permanent experiment.[40]

Technology has ceased to be simply technique, an instrument in the hands of man. It has created a new language which is not by any means restricted to the issues of know-how but speaks about a new hope for the liberation of history. Technology has become technologism, the starting point for a new type of humanism. The language of technologism is, indeed, the language of a new type of messianism: history will be liberated in and through the technological society.

What signs can the language of political humanism offer in order to vindicate itself? As against the achievements and wonders proclaimed by the language of technologism, it appears to be an almost absurd option. Would it not be the language of the romantics who think from their emotions and not from a realistic assessment of their resources? Would not the language of political humanism be like a cry of protest which finds its answer and fulfillment in a technological messianism? Why not abandon the cry and embrace the fulfillment? This option, however, has been stubbornly refused by those who speak the language of political humanism, although they seem to be unable to offer an alternate, more effective program than that presented by technologism. But why? Herbert Marcuse's *One-Dimensional Man* offers an articulate answer to this question. He suggests that the signs and wonders that the language of technologism presents as the ground for the hope of liberation, instead of making possible the creation of a new future by a free man, do just the opposite. Marcuse points out that in the so-called technological society technology is no longer the tool which, in the hands of free man, is necessary for the creation of a better world. It has rather become a system which envelops, conditions, and determines man. It is, indeed, creating a new type of man who has become one-dimensional and fat through the goods that the technological system creates. Man no longer simply uses technology; he is now a part of the total technological system. Consequently he is made incapable of critical thinking and action, futureless and ahistorical, at home in a system that is now his home and his permanent tomorrow. As we examine some aspects of the critique which the language of political humanism makes of the language of technologism, we must keep in mind that the critique is addressed not to technology in itself, but rather to totalitarian technological systems and the messianic pretensions of the language of technologism.

THE TECHNOLOGICAL SYSTEM AND THE DESTRUCTION OF NEGATION

Our previous analysis indicated that the language of political humanism is basically critical. Its critical character is derived from the fact that man, as a historical being, from his insertion into his historical present, apprehends it as suffering, futurelessness, impotence. The present has thus to be negated. In this act of negation man affirms both his historicity and his freedom, his transcendence over history. Only as a being not submerged in the facts, as one who is free from them, is he able to negate. The technological society, however, has succeeded in destroying this critical distance, by making man a part of it. Through its ability to deliver goods, it binds

> the consumers more or less pleasantly to the producers and, through the latter, to the whole. It is a good way of life—much better than before—and as a good way of life it militates against qualitative change. Thus emerges a pattern of one-dimensional thought and behavior in which ideas, aspirations and objectives that, by their content, transcend the established universe of discourse and action are either repelled or reduced to terms of this universe. They are redefined by the rationality of the given system and of its quantitative extension.[41]

When we discussed the results of colonialism on the colonial peoples we indicated that it was able to create an oppressed consciousness, that is, a consciousness which is domesticated and deprived of its futuricity. It did this by making the vision of the future impossible for the oppressed man. In the technological societies the same oppressed consciousness is again created but now for a different reason: because the future is no longer necessary. If the system gives or promises to give to man everything that he can dream of —and even that which is beyond his imagination—why should he remain opposed to it? The system does not cause him pain but rather pleasure. "The people [therefore] recognize themselves in their commodities; they find their soul in their automobile, hi-fi set, split-level home, kitchen equipment."[42] Technology creates a false man, a man who learns how to find happiness in what is given to him by the system. His soul is created as the image of what he can have. To the extent to which the system creates new needs and provides the objects to satisfy these needs, it is able to keep man an integral part of itself. Things traditionally opposed are now united. "Under the conditions of a rising standard of living," comments Marcuse, "non-conformity with the system itself appears to be socially useless."[43] Society acquires, accordingly, a totalitarian character with the disappearance of distance and opposition. The success of the system in the delivery of goods now provides the basis for the ideological justification and practical self-perpetuation. Whatever delivers goods must be true. Internal happiness requires defense against everything that is a threat from outside. Consequently, welfare state and warfare state become one, living in a harmonious symbiosis. "As the productive establishments rely on the military for self-preservation and growth, so the military relies on the corporations not only for their weapons, but also for the knowledge of what kind of weapons they need."[44]

The unity comes to a point where university and military research, investment in underdeveloped countries, and direct or indirect military intervention can no longer be considered objectively as separate issues. The system became global and in order to survive and expand it must remain global. Consequently its greatest enemy is that which negates it, that which stands over against it, that which refuses to become one of its integral parts.

In order to preserve an order of quantitative growth, the system must destroy the emergence of the qualitatively new.

> Neither the growing productivity nor the high standard of living depend on the threat from without, but their use for the containment of social change and perpetuation of servitude does. The Enemy is the common denominator of all doing and undoing. And the Enemy is not identical with actual communism or actual capitalism—he is, in both cases, the real spectre of liberation.[45]

In other words: the great enemy of the system is the critical distance, both in thought and action, that disrupts the ideological and functional totality of the integration of all opposites. The enemy, the "spectre of liberation," is the Negator, the political man who is not willing to trade his vocation as the creator of history for the role of consumer of goods. The system becomes thus the opiate of the people as it, by its ability to deliver goods on an increasing large scale, uses "the scientific conquest of nature for the scientific conquest of man."[46]

THE TECHNOLOGICAL SYSTEM AND THE END OF HOPE

Political humanism is a language of hope. Because of its radical criticism of the present, it considers society as unfinished. The new can and must be created. A new and better society is always possible. It therefore is commited to "naming the 'things that are absent.'" The universe of discourse of the technological society, however, does not make room for qualitative negation. Consequently it is not open for the new. "The way in which society organizes the life of its members," observes Marcuse, "involves an initial choice between historical alternatives. . . . It is one project among others. But once the project has become operative in the basic institutions and relations, it tends to become exclusive."[47] The system has its inner logic: the logic of quantity and extension—how to produce different, improved, or more things; how to expand; how to sell; how to boom; how to create new needs in man so that whatever the machine can produce can be sold. The future and hope are thus reduced to quantitative dimensions, to new forms of integration into the system, its logic and values.

This is the irony of technology: its functional excellence contributes to the preservation of the society into which it is inserted, its quantitative virtuousity creates qualitative immobility and its experimental and open-ended character solidifies the closedness of the society which it creates. It brings history to an end.

The opposition of political humanism to the messianic pretentions of technology is not, therefore, the expression of an unrealistic evaluation of its own possibilities but rather the result of its determination for the new in history. This is why many in the poor nations of the world are turning their backs on the affluent technocrats. They refuse to become parts of a system in which society becomes dominated by the inner logic of a system that does not make any room for the qualitatively new. This is why many students discover dimensions of dehumanization in a system that promises everything. They know that in order to become part of the system they have to "suppress the most creative impulses that they have." And this is why the black man refuses integration. Integration is the abdication of hope, as a critical category, before the triumphant logic of the technological society.

THE TECHNOLOGICAL SYSTEM AND THE DOMESTICATION OF ACTION

For political humanism action is to be the negation of the old and the creation of the new. Through this action man becomes the builder of history; history bears the stamp of his freedom. Technology, however, transforms creative behavior into operational behavior. The university becomes "a public utility serving the purely technical needs of society," "a factory for the production of knowledge and technicians to service the society's many bureaucracies." From creator of history man is transformed into one who perpetuates the given. No room is made for action which is transgression; it is to be functional. It manipulates quantities but is not allowed to give birth to the new. Therefore, "in the face of the totalitarian features of this society," Marcuse remarks, "the traditional notion of the 'neutrality' of technology can no longer be maintained. Technology as such cannot be isolated from the use to which it is put; the technological society is a system of domination."[48] It makes qualitative change impossible by making quantitative changes its mode of life.

When the dynamics of the technological society are seen from this angle, the idea of guaranteed income acquires some grim tones. What the prophets of technologism promise is that it will be possible for the man who always found his work a burden to have free time for the exercise of his creative possibilities. This may be true, to a great extent. But the other side must be taken into consideration: it will mean that the technological society no longer needs this man, that it is able to pay him to do nothing. He will be definitely separated from the heart of the system. The technological elites will be those who have the monopoly of power to create the future. Free time will be then the time of impotence, time of play, but not the time of creation. It will be the time of man as the object but never as the subject of history. He will be able to paint his pictures, to plant his garden, or to do anything he wants except to determine in any significant way the shape of his own future. I find, therefore, a great amount of truth in Marcuse's interpretation of the accomplishment of technological society.

> Our society distinguishes itself by conquering the centrifugal and social forces with Technology rather than Terror, on the dual basis of an overwhelming efficiency and an increasing standard of living. This containment of social change is perhaps the most singular achievement of advanced industrial society.[49]

It is true that containment of social change is perhaps the most singular achievement of advanced industrial society. However, it is not true that it does it with technology rather than with terror. Our present historical experience is somewhat different because we are confronting technology as terror. If in domestic relations technology conquers social change by the creation of happiness and elimination of pain as it delivers goods, in international relations the same containing impetus assumes an additional form: it conquers social change by the creation of death, destruction, and terror. One only needs to look at the military budgets of the powerful nations of the world to realize this. In the first case, it destroys social change by making consciousness closed to the future. In the second case, it achieves the same result by making the future closed to consciousness.

If we agree with van Leeuwen that technology was, in a certain sense, the mother of a new freedom for history, we must add now: like Saturn it devoured its own child.

The critique which the language of political humanism addresses to the language of technologism must not be understood as negation of technology. This would be nonsense. Political humanism does not want to destroy technology but rather to humanize it. And humanization of technology means that it must remain as a tool at the service of free subjects, as they are committed to the creation of a new tomorrow. Within the framework of the technological society this act of creation has been made impossible by the destruction of man as subject. Only when man is free, as the subject of his history, is technology a necessary instrument, but nothing more than an instrument, for the creation of a society and of a tomorrow in which man finds new forms of human liberation and fulfillment.

The Language of Political Humanism as a Critique of Theological Language

The language of political humanism is a new paradigm for humanization. It does not describe what is. It indicates what man must do in order to be human. Humanization is understood from man's relationship to history, as its object or subject, as created by it or as its creator.

The man who is the object of history, the being that fits in, that adapts to the given facts, is the man who loses his transcendence. He is submerged into the world and therefore loses his power to criticize and to re-create it. The positivity of the facts triumphs. This is why the messianism of technology is rejected: the technological society takes away from man his distance to negate, his openness to hope, his freedom to transgress. Materialism triumphs because the relations of production succeed in creating a man in their own image.[50]

Political humanism takes the second option. As we indicated before, this option is not derived from an ahistorical understanding of the nature of man. It is a historical decision, a historical risk. It is a decision to become a free subject. He is free as he negates the inhuman of the present, as he stretches his consciousness toward the exploration of the unfinished character of his world and names "the things which are absent," and makes his negation and hope historical through his action. Man's transcendence is thus the power that brings one day to its end and gives birth to the new one. The transcendent man lives thus between the times. Nay, the times are divided between the untruth which is left behind and the truth toward which one moves because man is in history. Transcendence thus takes shape historically. Only as an historical being is man able to negate and to hope. And only as a being that transcends history is he able to create a new history, the history of his freedom. Transcendence is thus future directed. The higher realization of truth toward which this consciousness stretches itself is to be found in a new tomorrow. The new future is its beyond, its determination and love.

The most common language of the churches, however, discloses the fact that the consciousness which speaks it has a radically different structure. John A. T. Robinson observes that ecclesiastical language is rather determined by "ups" and "outs." It either refers to transcendence as something which "is literally or physically up there, or as a spiritual or metaphysical reality which is out there."[51]

This language does not understand transcendence as a reality in the midst of life, which creates history. It rather separates between time and eternity, between transcendence and history. Transcendence becomes a truth higher than, above, and beyond history. Consciousness, consequently, does not stretch itself toward a new tomorrow but rather attempts to move upwards, toward the experience of a transcendent realm beyond matter and time, the spiritual and eternal sphere. It creates religion as the house of the transcendent. It becomes the stable and fixed amid the historical process.

The structure of the consciousness of political humanism, however, does not have room for this type of transcendence. It is totally secular, born out of history, committed to history. Its ethical exigency, its categorical imperative for the transformation of the world is not derived from a beyond but rather from its historical character, its insertion into its present, its participation in the sufferings of the human community, which is its sole point of reference. Both the exigency of the situation and the resources available for the task are totally human and secular. We find here a man who, in the words of Bonhoeffer, "has learned to cope with all questions of importance without recourse to God as a working hypothesis."[52]

When we understand the structural difference between these two types of consciousness, one that sees transcendence as inserted into history and the other that believes it to be beyond history, we come to realize the problems involved as we attempt to have a dialogue between them. The language of theology and of the Church, the language of many hymns, liturgies, and sermons sounds to the secular man who is committed to the task of creating a new world like the voice of an alien and remote sphere. This is one of the reasons why a growing number of people are leaving the churches and opting for a totally secular humanism.[53] It seems that in the confrontation between the two languages one is led to the conclusion that in order to be free for history and for the transformation of society one has to unlearn the language of theology. One does not see how it is possible to be faithful to one's vocation as the creator of history, on the one hand, and as a member of a community which takes man out of history and pushes him into a meta-historical sphere, on the other. Obviously their allegiance shifts to the communities where a common language of concern for human liberation in history is spoken. They very soon come to realize the greatness of those "who do not first seek behind the stars for a reason to go under and be a sacrifice, but who sacrifice themselves for the earth."[54]

The problem of the conflict between the two languages is more serious than it seems. The issue is not that they are different languages. If that were so, it would be possible to achieve a dialogue and conversation between them by the simple process of learning the other language. The fact, however, is that they seem to be rather structurally opposed in such a way that the true learning of one, that is, the apprehension of the historical experience which it carries with itself, requires the unlearning of the other. Today, however, in the atmosphere of "dialogue," the sharp edges tend to be forgotten in the attempt to achieve a common ground for conversation. I do not believe that this is healthy because it prevents a true confrontation, a shock, which could become the occasion for radical self-criticism on both sides and therefore for a new historical experience which could make man freer than he was before. A true dialogue thus requires full awareness of the radical opposition.

It seems to me that this opposition is nowhere indicated in a more forcible and passionate manner than in the writings of Nietzsche. He welcomed the death of God—and with it the end of theological language—as a joyful and liberating reality.

> We feel as if a new dawn were shining on us when we receive the tidings that "the old god is dead"; our heart overflows with gratitude, amazement, anticipation, expectation. At last the horizon appears free again to us, even granted that it is not bright; at last our ships may venture out again, venture out to face new dangers; all the daring of the lover of knowledge is permitted again; the sea, our sea, lies open again.[55]

Notice how the death of God is the counterpart of a new freedom for the earth, for the future: "Our ships may venture out again . . ." If the death of God means the liberation of man it is because the life of God implies the bondage of man. He was the restraining wall, the limitation of freedom, the domestication of man's daring and creativity—at least the God about whom the language of the Church spoke. We have to read Nietzsche as poetry and prophetic imagination. It does not matter if his description is not scientific and accurate in detail. What is important is that his language is like a magnifying glass through which what we cannot see as inhuman is presented in naked brutality as what is crooked and ugly. He paints the God of the language of the Church as the anti-human, and those who speak that language as those who perpetuate inhumanity.

> Here are the priests; and though they are my enemies, pass by them silently and with sleeping swords. . . . They have called "God" what was contrary to them and gave them pain. . . . And they did not know how to love their god except by crucifying man. . . . Whoever lives near them lives near black ponds out of which an ominous frog sings its song with sweet melancholy. They would have to sing better songs for me to learn to have faith in their Redeemer: and his disciples would have to look more redeemed![56]

Nietzsche is pointing out that the Christian language about transcendence expressed an experience that emptied the body, the senses, freedom, creativity, of their validity and beauty and denied them in the name of another world. Therefore the glorification of God corresponded to the suffering and annihilation of man. His was the name which expressed "that hatred against everything human, even more, against everything animal, everything material, . . . disgust with the senses, with reason itself, . . . fear of happiness and beauty, [a] desire to get away from all semblance, change, and becoming,"[57] that is, the negation of history and the world as the home of man. Therefore life comes to an end where "the kingdom of God begins."[58] Feuerbach makes the same charges against the language of theology: "The impoverishment of the real world and the enriching of God is one act. Only the poor man has a rich God. God springs out of the feeling of want. . . . God is the compensation for the poverty of life. . . . [He] is to religion the substitute for the lost world."[59]

It is obvious that there is difference between them. For Nietzsche God is the cause of man's suffering; he makes man suffer. For Feuerbach God is a compensation for man's suffering; he is man's suffering and want projected as happiness and richness. For both, however, the result is the same, since God does not allow man to overcome his misery, either because he causes it or because he reconciles man with it, by giving him the hope of a transcendent, meta-historical liberation. Suffering and misery become then the permanent house of man. If God causes man's suffering or liberates him meta-historically from it, suffering loses its character of contradiction that is to be overcome by action. The negative becomes the positive and men are led to "recognize and acknowledge as a concession of heaven the very fact that they are mastered, ruled, possessed!"[60]

Political humanism remains irreconciled with the negativity of history. The negative must be negated. If God transforms the negative into a positive, then belief in God forbids man to negate what is destroying him. God is then the negation of the consciousness of political humanism. The conflict between the two languages is obvious. The negation of the negative cannot be in dialogue with the positivization of the negative.

Nietzsche points out another inhumanity of theological languages: God is the end of history. He is the "One and the Plenum and the Unmoved and the Sated and the Permanent."[61] The world is that which is unreal; God is reality. But God is finished, ready. How could man find his vocation in the creation of the world, if the world is unreal? And how could he ever create something new, if everything is already finished in God? When man sets his mind on God he at once loses his world and his freedom to create. It is this man who is the great danger for history. "Who represents the greatest danger for all of man's future?" he asks. "Is it not the good and just? Inasmuch as they say and feel in their hearts, 'We already know what is good and just, and we have it too.' . . . The noble man wants to create something new and a new virtue. The good wants the old, and that the old be preserved."[62] The sin of the good man is the same sin of the bureaucrats of the technological society. They believe that history has ended. If God contains all values, man cannot create the new. He is to fit in, to repeat the old. History, instead of marching toward ever new horizons, becomes directed toward the past. Man's transcendence is not creation but adaptation. He does not know that through his virtues of repetition he was turned from a wolf into a dog, into a domestic animal.[63] God, thus, is not freedom for man. He is the domestication of man, the end of the "homo creator."

When the death of God is proclaimed, obviously man is made free again for his world, for history, for creation. The world is desacralized. Its frozen values thaw. Nothing is final. The horizons become permission and invitation. Man is free for experimentation. The truth of the world is established;[64] man is now free to make it his home. He is liberated from the burden of the past and made free for the future. From his hope he is free to recreate his world from his love and freedom. The earth, the body, the senses are now delightful gifts, occasions for joy and celebration.

The rediscovery of the truth of the earth carries with itself the discovery of man's vocation. His task: to give a human meaning to the earth.[65] A very humble task: one abdicates the pretension to scale the walls of eternity. Man's freedom and transcendence are now turned to the task of transforming the earth "into a site of recovery" for man. The present is lived for the sake of the future of man.[66] The "homo creator," the man who lives for the sake of the future, is born when the language that sacralized and paralyzed the present comes to an end. The language of political humanism is thus radically opposed to any language which, in the name of any truth higher than the human, makes man at home in the inhumanity of his present. Religion, therefore, is to be destroyed for the sake of the earth, for the sake of man's freedom to criticize his world in order to transform it. "Thus, the criticism of heaven turns into the criticism of the earth, the criticism of religion into the criticism of right and the criticism of theology into the criticism of politics."[67] The criticism of heaven, religion, and theology is the negation of a presence beyond history which claims that, without the mediation of man's action, the negativity of the present is eliminated. Consciousness does not find therefore in God a resting place. It remains restless between its present which it has to negate, and the hope for a new future which can be created.[68]

As we indicated before, political humanism is a paradigm for humanization. It is dominated by the passion and vision of human liberation. Its historical commitment indicates what it understands to be human and what are the available resources for this task. What its critique of theological language indicates is that it does not see that the two languages belong to the same world, refer to the same man, and are concerned with the same task of creating a new tomorrow for mankind. If we are not really committed to the task of making man more free, historically, then our task ends here. There is no basis for further reflection. We go back to our traditional language and remain safe within its limits. If, on the contrary, we love the earth, the concrete man, and the future that can be created, we have ahead of us two tasks. First, to inquire about the truth of the criticism which political humanism makes of the language of the community of faith. And second, to explore the positive resources that the historical experience of the community of faith could offer for the task of historical human liberation. We now turn to an examination of some of the languages of the community of faith and the paradigms for human liberation they contain, from the perspective of the criticism that political humanism addresses to them.

THE EXISTENTIALIST LANGUAGE: "TRUTH AS SUBJECTIVITY"

Existentialism has a great affinity with political humanism. Both of them affirm that man cannot remain human if he ceases to be a subject in history. As political humanism is a protest against the powers that recreate man in their image and likeness, thereby destroying him as a subject, existentialism is a protest against the powers of "massification" that bring man's freedom to an end. For both of them man's life swings between two possibilities: either freedom from the world and with it authentic existence, or falling into the hypnotic grasp of the power of the world and the inauthentic existence it entails.

Existentialism is thus the expression of the profound concern for man's freedom from the world, for his transcendence, for the preservation of his authentically human character, and a radical opposition to everything that means the loss of the uniqueness of the existing individual into anything that submerges or engulfs him. This is the central reason why Kierkegaard rejects the

Hegelian system. Hegel's philosophy transformed the individual into a simple accident within the total historical process. The truth of history was the truth of the process and only to the extent that the individual was in the process did his existence participate in truth. Kierkegaard could not see, however, any truth higher than that of the individual and of subjectivity. "Truth is subjectivity" he proclaims. And from this basic conviction he inveighs against all the structures—philosophical, political, and religious—which had absolved man from the central demand of "salvation," namely, the task of becoming an individual.

In Heidegger's analysis of *Dasein* we find again the same understanding of the structure of the inauthentic and of the authentic life. He indicates that when man "is fascinated by the world" and absorbed by it he falls into a mode of life which is inauthentic because then man loses himself. Indeed, he can be described as "being lost in the publicness of the 'they,' "[69] of the impersonal into which man is now submerged. Existentialism, therefore, in its concern for the freedom of man from the world that surrounds him, altogether agrees with the protest of political humanism against the structures of the technological society that create the one-dimensional man, or the structures of colonialism that do not allow man to be a free subject in history. Both paradigms make a similar diagnosis of what is making man inhuman in the world. They part ways, however, when they indicate "what it takes to make and to keep human life human in the world." Political humanism invites man to be the creator of history. It believes that an authentic existence can transform the world, creating it in the image and likeness of its own freedom. The inhumanity of the structures that make man inhuman must be destroyed by an act of this same man. By his power he penetrates into the today which domesticates and from his action a new tomorrow is created. This tomorrow is to be the reconciliation between the existential and the world, between the subjective and the objective, since it is a child of man's authentic life. Political humanism believes, thus, that man's action is able to reconcile and unite man, as free and transcendent, with his world. Humanization, therefore, requires the aggressiveness of man's subjectivity. It must become an act. Through an act whereby subjec-

tivity invades the world of space and time, man is able to create a
break in history, to produce a qualitative change in time, which is,
indeed, the event of the birth of the new.

Existentialism, however, points to a different solution, because
one of its most basic presuppositions is the irreconcilability between the subjective and the objective. Transcendence and freedom are always separated from the objective by an "infinite
qualitative difference." It accepts the divided world of Kantian
philosophy. On the one hand is the world of time, of the objective,
of scientific reason, the profane, phenomenal world. On the other
hand is the world of freedom, of eternity, of God, of transcendence,
the noumenal world. This is the basic polarity—and why not say
"split"?—that informs Kierkegaard's thought. Consequently his
thought moves in the sphere of a radical asceticism regarding everything that means time or objective. He cannot take history seriously. History, a category of time, cannot provide any clues for the
transcendent beyond time. "Nothing historical can become infinitely certain for me," he proclaims, "except the fact of my own
existence and this is not something historical."[70] If we put freedom
and the historical within the same language we cannot avoid breaking all the rules of logical thought. This conjunction will appear as
what can be objectively described only as "absurd"[71] and which
cannot be expressed save through the language of paradox.[72] This
radical discontinuity indicates how impossible it is for existentialist
thought to conceive of transcendence as making an impact upon
time, as changing the structures of time and creating thereby a new
time, as political humanism does. The transcendent remains always
"elusive,"[73] a shadow that never becomes history.

This same dualism runs through Bultmann's interpretation of
the Gospel, as a paradigm of humanization. His theology starts
from a deeply missionary concern. In his dialogue with modern
man, the man who speaks the language of science, Bultmann is
aware that he lives in a different world from that of the New
Testament. "The kerygma is incredible to modern man," he declares, "for he is convinced that the mythical view of the world is
obsolete." And he asks: "Can Christian preaching expect modern

man to accept the mythical view of the world as true?"[74] To do so would be both "senseless and impossible."

The alternative is obvious: either the Gospel became out-moded with the mythological view of the world of the New Testament and should therefore be abandoned, or the Gospel is not related to a worldview. If the Gospel is not related to a worldview the task of theology is then "demythologization," that is, to liberate it from the wrong frame of reference and to translate it into categories of the right frame of reference. Bultmann opts for the categories provided by the "existentialist interpretation as the only solution."[75] This means basically that the message of the Gospel as the message of and for the liberation of man has to do exclusively with the subjective, existential sphere. The world remains outside the grasp of transcendence. How is it possible to speak about transcendence in the world if the historical experience of man is not one of liberation but of bondage? "Those who have endured the hardships of a Russian prison camp know better than anyone else that you cannot say *Terra ubique Domini* as an explicit dogma"; the truth is that "the whole world is profane."[76] How is it possible to make room for God in a world which is closed within the limits of scientific reason and dominated by causal relationships, the world indeed which makes no room for freedom, as Kant indicated? The impossibility of speaking about God and transcendence in conjunction with the objective world is what makes "the existentialist interpretation the only solution," because the existential sphere has the possibility of remaining free from the world of causality. The "existential" is thus the locus of transcendence and it is with it that the task of human liberation has to do.

When transcendence is understood in terms of the "infinite qualitative difference between time and eternity," of the irreconciliable split between the world of freedom, existential and subjective, and the world of objective structures, man has to abdicate the vocation to create, out of his freedom and transcendence, a new tomorrow. Borrowing from Barth one of the images that he used in his first phase, we could say that man's transcendence and freedom always remain tangential to the world of time and space, touching it but never taking shape in it. Politics, thus, can never be the answer to the question "what does it take to make and to keep human life human in the world?" The answer is found somewhere else.

The existentialist answer to the problem of humanization corresponds to its analysis of the human self. The human self is a mirror that reflects both worlds, freedom and necessity. It exists in between, stretched between the infinite and the finite, attracted by the vocation to be free but at the same time "fascinated by the world." "Man," Kierkegaard observes, "is a synthesis of the infinite and the finite, of the temporal and of the eternal, of freedom and necessity." But since finitude and infinitude, the temporal and the eternal, are infinitely apart, the synthesis is not a synthesis. It is a "process of becoming," a "moving away from oneself infinitely by the process of infinitizing oneself, and in returning to oneself infinitely by the process of finitizing"[77] in such a way that the self cannot ever attain equilibrium and rest.

The existing individual is thus divided between two possibilities: he either remains transcendent over the world, existing authentically, or he falls prey of objectivity, losing thereby his freedom and existing inauthentically. In this polarity we find both man's possibility of existing authentically and of being lost. It is the transcendence which belongs ontologically to his self that makes him aware of his finite pole. Because he is transcendent, he is aware that he is a "being-towards-death."[78] This means despair (Kierkegaard) or anxiety (Heidegger). Man, therefore, cannot avoid caring about security. It is as man tries to find security that he is either going to be truly human through the risk of freedom, or will be lost in the structures of the world in which he mistakenly thought that he could save himself from death.

The temptation is to make the decision for the objective. Man is deceived when he thinks that the quantitative promises of the world are able to transpose the qualitative abyss that separates transcendence from time. He opts for objective security. But when he does this he becomes like a dancer who, from his ability to jump very high, wants to make the others and himself believe that he is able to fly! He becomes "comical"[79] as he makes the infinite passion

Jeanne E. Magrath

of his inwardness rest on an object that is finite. It is this same man whom Bultmann describes as the one who trusts in his own works. What he does, his performance, is the ground of his security. In man's "care" lurks a self-reliant attitude which believes that the problem of "care" will be solved through its power to dispose of the world. But when it does this "it factually falls victim to the world." Man then loses his freedom, his authenticity. He is under "slavery" and his freedom gives place now to the fear which haunts all the spheres of his life.

The objective world is thus a threat, the world into which man falls, the world which seduces and objectivizes him. It is never man's home. Rather he finds himself thrown into it. Consequently he will become human only to the extent that he will make the decision not to be "fascinated"[80] by it. This opposition between man and the world is the central motif of the writings of Kafka. Man is pictured in his fear and hopelessness as he is caught by the impersonal bureaucracy-like structures of the world. There are no possibilities left. Man cannot choose between running away or confronting the powers behind the bureaucracies. There are no options because there are no exits. And because there are no exits there is no hope.

We meet again the same element we indicated before: the strangeness of freedom and transcendence in the world of time and space. The world cannot and will not be a home for man. The project of humanization, therefore, cannot be understood as the transformation of the world by man and for man. It is rather man's liberation of himself from the world.

The paradigm for the liberation of man offered by existentialism is, consequently, necessarily subjective. To become human is to become subjectively free. Humanization is subjectivization because "subjectivity is truth, subjectivity is reality."[81] The event of humanization does not leave marks on the earth! It is the shift from an old self-understanding in which man found his security in performance, to a new one in which he renounces his self-achieved assurance and becomes free from the bondage of the world.[82] The immediate consequence of the totally subjective character of humanization, as a new self-understanding, is that the objective is dismissed as totally devoid of significance and import for the task of making the human life human in the world. Kierkegaard, for instance, as he declares that "salvation" has only to do with the "how" of subjectivity, adds also that the objective has no reality. It is indeed the "how"[83] of subjectivity which determines the contents of reality. "It is the passion of the infinite that is the decisive factor and not the content," he says, "for its content is precisely itself."[84]

If humanization is the same thing as the emergence of a new subjectivity, the passionate subjectivity, the new self-understanding, we have now to ask: what is the method for this task? How can man be involved in the liberation of man? The task is clear: to induce a new self-understanding. But this cannot be directly communicated.[85] Kierkegaard consequently sees his task as making the "whats" more and more elusive, in such a way as to provoke in the hearer, by induction, the passion that cannot be reduced to words. Or, with Bultmann, the instrument of humanization is the preaching of the Word that proclaims the event which calls man to decision, to a new self-understanding. It is when subjectivity is touched, induced to passion, or led to a decision of faith that the event of transcendence occurs. The instrument for humanization, therefore, is not to be measured by its power to create a new tomorrow, but by its power to touch man's subjectivity.

The import of the event of this new self-understanding is that man is de-historized. He is taken from the relations of determination that surround him in the world of time and space. The deed of God, the event of transcendence "lifts man out of his worldly ties and places him directly before His own eyes." This act is "the de-historization" or the "de-secularization both of God and man." ". . . God, who stands aloof from the history of nations, meets each man in his own little history, his everyday life with its daily gift and demand; de-historized man (i.e., naked of his supposed security within his historical group) is guided into his concrete encounter with his neighbor, in which he finds his true history."[86] The same is true for Kierkegaard. In the event of the infinite passion, the reality of the transcendent is made present, thereby destroying space and time, determinations that are the framework of the world and history. Transcendence is thus the end of time; eschatological existence (Bultmann) is existence lived before the eternal Now.

This statement seems to be in open contradiction to what Bultmann himself says about the relationship between faith and hope, which is a determination of the self for time.

> "Faith" is no self-contained condition of man's soul, but points toward the future . . . [Thus] "Faith" is also "hope" . . . This "hope" is the freedom for the future and the openness toward it which the man of faith has because he has turned over his anxiety about himself and his future to God in obedience.[87]

Once more I would like to indicate the similarity between the existentialist analysis and that of political humanism. Political humanism speaks about a new self-understanding on the part of man which makes him free from the given structures of the past, structures that became law, and free for a new future, a future which is "not yet" and a "risk." Structurally these are dimensions of freedom created by faith. However, there is a radical opposition between them. Let us hear what Bultmann himself says:

> . . . [Jesus'] proclamation of the will of God must be described as an eschatological ethic. For it does not envisage a future to be molded within this world by plans and sketches for the ordering of human life. It only directs man into the Now of his meeting with his neighbor.[88]

This statement deserves our attention. Bultmann had declared that faith makes man open for the future. Faith is thus hope. Now he declares that the eschatological event has nothing to do with a historical future but only with the Now. How is it possible to have in the act of faith both the de-historization of man, his liberation from time, and at the same time, his liberation for a future which, however, has nothing to do with a historical future, but only with the eschatological Now? The answer is simple. The event of transcendence really de-historizes man. The freedom for the future that Bultmann speaks about is a mode of the subjectivity, an "ecstasis of *Dasein*" (Heidegger). It has to do with the openness of subjectivity. The other side of the coin, however, is that the future is not open for man. The historical future remains profane, secular. The act of God changes man's self-understanding; man is now free for the future. It has nothing to do, however, with time. The future is not free for man. As we indicated before, a new future is impossible within the existentialist paradigm, since transcendence is not inserted into history and the world by man's freedom, but remains circumscribed by the sphere of subjectivity. It seems that we are confronted here with a new type of fictionism: man lives as if the future were open to him, knowing, however, that it is not. As a consequence, Bultmann shows himself to be totally unconcerned about the problem of efficacy. The important is not the "what" but the "that" (the same polarity between "what" and "how" in Kierkegaard). The neighbor ceases to be an historical being, living within the determination of time and space. Political humanism would say: I love man and I know that man lives in the world, is determined by it. Therefore, because I love my neighbor who lives today, I have to create a new world in which he will be freer tomorrow. To this, however, Bultmann says:

> The demand for love needs no formulated stipulations; the example of the merciful Samaritan shows that a man can know and must know what he has to do when he sees his neighbor in need of his help. The little words "as yourself" in the love-commandment pre-indicate both the boundlessness and the direction of loving conduct. . . . That fact shows that his proclamation of the will of God is not an ethic of world-reform.[89]

We cannot lose sight of the objective of these reflections on existentialism. We are examining, on the one hand, the congruity between the historical project to which Christians and communities of non-Christians are committed, for creating a new future for man and, on the other, the resources offered by our theological language for such a task. We are thus exploring the relationships between a project of humanization which is political in character, and the possible resources that our most common paradigms for humanization offer. This is why we examined some of the aspects of existentialism, in their relation to our problem.

We can summarize our conclusions, using the three basic determinations of the political consciousness as a framework.

1. Political humanism negates the inhuman of the present structures and their dehumanizing power for the sake of a better tomorrow. It negates the world today because it loves the world, because it wants to transform it into a home, into "a site of recovery." Existentialism, on the contrary, simply and flatly negates the world. In the world a new tomorrow is never possible. Man can never feel at home in it. The possible changes in the world have nothing whatsoever to do with the issue of humanization and dehumanization. We could say that there is in existentialism something of Marcionism: a despair about the created world whereas the event of humanization is divorced from it.

2. Political humanism has hope for a new future. Because man is open for the future, man can make the future open for himself. His hope is, therefore, historical. It has to do with the world and with time. It secularizes and historizes man. Existentialism, however, because of its despair about the world, reduces hope to a dimension of subjectivity, without any import for the transformation of the world. Its hope does not create but abrogates history.

3. Political humanism understands man as "homo creator": he has the "power" to insert his transcendence into space and time. His transcendence becomes act, history. It creates the new, thereby making possible the reconciliation between the existential and the objective, since the tomorrow is to bear the stamp of man's negation and hope. Political humanism, therefore, wants to push the existentialist passion for and vision of authentic life to its utmost possibilities. It wants to see authentic life, free subjectivity, creating a new tomorrow, a new time, a new world. This is why it comes into conflict with the existentialist, ultimate division between the world of freedom and the world of time and space. In the context of this division man's action becomes powerless to create a new tomorrow. It remains a flash of the Eternal Now in time, always tangential, always impotent to fertilize the earth.

Existentialism, therefore, although in many ways a very rich and helpful paradigm for humanization, does not offer the resources necessary for a project of political nature. A new paradigm of humanization and therefore a new language of faith are required.

THE BARTHIAN PARADIGM: FROM THE "NO" OF CRISIS TO THE "YES" OF ELECTION

Our task now is to explore the possible contribution of the language created by K. Barth for the political project of human liberation to which many Christians and Christian communities are committed. The procedure will be the same adopted in our conversation with existentialism. We will confront the Barthian language, asking: How do you answer the question "What does it take to make and to keep human life human in the world?" What is your paradigm for humanization? And then we will try to see in which ways its answer could prove helpful to the project which understands humanization as related to the creation of a new future for man.

Crisis. The situation that gave birth to the Barthian language was the conflict between the optimistic expectations of nineteenth-century liberalism and the hard realities of the historical experience brought about by World War I. The expectations of technological progress, of human liberation, of the triumph of man's reason over the irrational and instinctive in history, the assurance that man had liberated himself from the tutelage of the political and religious heteronomous powers—all the hopes and certainties that were implied in Kant's proclamation[90] of man come of age—were confronted with a radical and unexpected No. The optimism of the language of progress as the paradigm for human liberation could not survive the hard language of the facts: history did not have immanent in its process the power to make human life human.

Barth discovered, at the same time, that there was much more realism in the language of the Bible than in the language of nineteenth-century liberalism. The Bible did not speak about progress. It was rather deeply aware of the self-destructive potentialities of human creativity. The destruction of the hopes of progressive self-liberation, therefore, could be better understood from the perspective of "the strange world of the Bible."[91] This is why Barth declares that "a wide reading of contemporary secular literature—especially of newspapers—is . . . recommended to any one desirous of understanding the Epistle of the Romans."[92] Both the language of the Bible and the language of the papers pointed to the same fact: history is not the bearer of humanization; it cannot offer any messianic promises; its gift is rather despair, frustration, and the destruction of man.

Barth's theological enterprise, as a consequence, took the shape of what he himself called an "antiseptic task";[93] it aimed at the creation of a language that would be free from the false hopes created by an uncritical understanding of man and history. As there could not be any hope of humanization at the expense of the truth about history and its frustrating negativity, so the task of creating a new paradigm for humanization was first of all destructive: the false paradigm, the false answer to the question "what does it take to make and to keep human life human in the world?" had to be shown to be an illusion. Barth came to realize that there would not be any hope for man except in the context of the hopelessness of history. Humanization, therefore, could not be seen as a gift of history. It would come from that which was beyond history and negated it.

Barth's paradigm for humanization is thus radically critical, whence the title "theology of crisis" given to it. It must be noted, however, that Barth did not see his attempt to create a new theological language merely as a fruit of disappointment with history. He believed that his critical stand was basically biblical and theological and not the mere result of critical analysis. Theologically and biblically there was no basis whatsoever for the messianization of history and man. The possibility of human liberation was from God's side, it was God's gracious gift. This God, however, in whom all the hopes of human fulfillment rested, was radically beyond history. With Kierkegaard he repeated that there was an "infinite qualitative difference" between God and man, eternity and time. Because "revelation is not a predicate of history,"[94] humanization is not one of its immanent possibilities. Everything the world and history present to us "in the last resort . . . [does] not point us to God, but to ourselves, to our God alienated souls."[95] We can know neither God nor ourselves and our destiny by starting from the world and history. God cannot be apprehended either by means of pious feelings (Schleiermacher), history (Hegel and Baur), or in the moral consciousness (Kant, Ritschl). He remains hidden, beyond history, as the "Wholly Other." The reality of God is thus basically separation, opposition, negation. The total otherness of God remains as such even in the event of revelation. "This hiddenness," says Barth, "completely contrary to nature as it is, is a necessary determination of revelation."[96] One cannot, thus, speak unequivocally about the presence of God. He "is to be seen as the invisible and expressed only as the inexpressible."[97] Our words about God are to portray the "elusiveness" of God, since "the being apprehended by us in thoughts and words is always either not yet or else no longer the being of God."[98] This has to be so because God is opposed to history and time. The dialectic of thought is thus the mirror of the tangential character of revelation, which touches the world and history but which never becomes world and history.

As we mentioned before, the influence of the Kantian and Kierkegaardian understanding of transcendence was basic to this paradigm. Transcendence does not penetrate into history but stands over against it. It is time in its totality, the world in its totality, human creativity in its totality, historical hopes in their totality that receive the radical No of God. God's freedom from time issues into God's negation of time. We find in Barth a "more metaphysical sense of the crisis of all humanity before God,"[99] comments C. C. West. The historical and negative are thus identified. With Bultmann, Barth could have said that revelation is the dehistorization and de-secularization of God and man. His theology of transcendence is therefore a radical form of negative thinking: everything which is time and world is negated since in their own being as time, as world, as history, as man, they are opposed to and negated by God. As we confront God "we stand . . . [therefore] before an irresistible and all embracing dissolution of the world of time and things of man, before a penetrating and ultimate *Krisis,* before the supremacy of a negation by which all existence is rolled up."[100] This radical negation becomes, as a consequence, the critical tool by means of which we come to know what history and human creativity really are:

> The display of the supposed advantages of power and intelligence which some men possess over others, of the struggle for existence hypocritically described by the ideologists as a struggle for justice and freedom, of the ebb and flow of old and new

forms of human righteousness, each vying with the rest in solemnity and triviality.[101]

Order! What is the existing order? . . . a new strengthening and defense of man against God; a securing of the normal course of the world . . . a conspiracy of the far too many against the One. What legality is not illegal at heart? What authority is not tyranny?[102]

Is this the end of history *and* the end of man? Is not this metaphysical negation at its roots the theological justification of nihilism? Barth did not think so and did not intend to have his thought thus understood. The negation existed for the sake of the affirmation. The fact of the negation, indeed, pointed to the transcendent ground from which it came, the "beyond" which, exactly by the fact that it denied the negativity of history, constituted another reality, the reality of God, the ground of hope for man. "This No," comments Barth in relation to the cross, "is a No which cannot be ignored or contradicted, a divine No which reposes upon the divine Yes of revelation. . . ."[103] The cross reveals what the highest in man's piety and order can do. They negate the Son of God and with him, man. The cross, therefore, is the end of history, it is the revelation of the impiety which lurks behind everything that occurs in time. But the cross as negation does not remain the last word. The resurrection follows it. And the resurrection is the impossible possibility, impossible because the possibilities of history were exhausted on the cross. But possible because God's grace operates exactly when the possibilities of history come to an end. The divine Yes of revelation is thus found in the resurrection which is the triumphant Yes that negates the cross and opens the way to the possibility that God's grace creates. God's possibility, the new aeon, has thus conquered the negativity of history, although the reality of this negated time still remains.[104] But it remains only for a while, because that last word has already been pronounced by God in his affirmation of the "wholly other" reality which the resurrection inaugurated.

We do not need to say how this polarity between the No and the Yes can be helpful for the project of creating a new future for man. We are confronted here with that basic structural polarity which we found in our analysis of the consciousness of political humanism: the critical negation of "what is" is what creates the hope for what "can be" but which is "not yet." It is when transcendence inserts itself into history that the negation of the old and the creation of the new is made possible. Transcendence thus mediates the new into history, through the creation of a new tomorrow.

Barth, however, did not allow for this possibility. He realized that some could use his dialectic between negation and affirmation as a critical tool for the transformation of the world. But he flatly denied that this was his intention. More than that: he denied that his theology could make room for this sort of conclusion.

> It is not unlikely that its [*The Epistle to the Romans*] reading may foster a contempt for the present order and an attitude of negation towards it. The disquiet, the questioning, the negation, the emphatic insistence upon the parable of death, to which Christianity is definitely committed (XII.6), may be so misunderstood as to be transformed into a positive method of human behavior, into a means of justification, indeed, into the Titanism of revolt and upheaval and renovation. The revolutionary Titan is far more godless, far more dangerous than his reactionary counterpart.[105]

An amazing statement! There is more godlessness in the attempt to create a new tomorrow for man than in the acritical affirmation of the present that destroys man! Why? The answer is found in Barth's concept of transcendence. Transcendence is the negation that stands over against the whole world, the whole of history. It is the transcendence which, as it affirms itself, negates the world. It creates an either/or alternative. It is not transcendence for the sake of the world, transcendence committed to making and keeping human life human in the world. On the contrary: the humanization created by the "wholly other" is rather related to the dehistorization of man, the "taking away of our time."[106] Humanization expresses itself in the creation of a consciousness that is permanently in exile in this world, a world that is never home, as with existentialism. God's salvation is thus the end of history: it creates "in history a horror at history."[107] The hope that God's revelation inaugurated is accordingly not only meta-historical but anti-historical. This has to be so because history, as time and space, cannot ever make room for humanization.

The result of this docetic transcendence is the sense of futility which then dominates human action. As with Kafka, there is no way out. Human creativity cannot create a new tomorrow because the hope that God's negation offers does not point to a new tomorrow in history. The fact is that "the judgment of God is the end of history, not the beginning of a new, a second epoch. By it history is not prolonged but done away with."[108] All the options are equally rejected. "Reaction and revolution," comments Barth, "have always drawn their nourishment from the same source, the one in fear, the other in desire, and both in Godlessness."[109]

What is left for man to do? What is the paradigm left for the task of making and keeping human life human in the world? To the extent that the world is negated, human life in the world is really human life that rejects the world, that finds its home in another sphere, as it happened with existentialism. Humanization, therefore, has nothing to do with the "homo creator"—the Titan!—and the creation of a new tomorrow. The result of this position, Dr. West indicates, is that from the perspective of Barth's paradigm of humanization "the Christian must not allow himself to be distracted by changes in political order or by the relative struggles for power in history from the primary task of proclaiming the reconciliation of man and God in Christ."[110] We thus find our hope in a meta-historical reality announced by the word and tangential to the world: it does not offer the critical tools for the task of creating a new tomorrow. Humanization is a function of the right hearing of the word and not of the critical transformation of history. We should ask if this paradigm for humanization does not function as the opiate of the people!

The "Yes" of Election. Barth himself realized that this paradigm for humanization was, at the bottom, profoundly inhuman. In his article "The Humanity of God" he mentions the "somewhat cruelly inhuman" character and implications of his former understanding of transcendence. The expressions that pointed to the radical separation and opposition between God and the world— such as the "infinite qualitative difference," "the vertical from

above," the "vacuum," the "mathematical point," the "tangent"—
were inhuman in that they did not start from the reality of Jesus
Christ, God with us and for us.[111] They had their source rather in
the philosophies of Kant and Kierkegaard. God's transcendence
cannot be understood from the perspective of an abstract "wholly
other," but only from the realization that God's transcendence is
a different name for "the humanity of God." It is true that anthropology cannot be the starting point for theology. But it is also
certainly true for the Christian faith that God is only known as man.
It is true that revelation is not a predicate of history; but it must
nevertheless be said that "the word of God in the highest sense
makes history."[112] Transcendence becomes history, world, time.
The word, says Barth "does not remain transcendent over time, it
does not merely meet it at a point, but it enters time; nay, it assumes
time; nay, it creates time for itself."[113] And what makes transcendence historical is God's freedom, which becomes act. The act of
God is, thus, what mediates between him and the world. God acts
and the world changes; signs, in the form of creaturely objectivity,
appear.[114]

We see here a substantial change in Barth's paradigm for humanization. Previously the hope of human liberation went together
with the total negation of the world. Now God's transcendence,
instead of negating the world to man, gives it to him as permission.
This shift was possible because Barth realized that God's transcendence over man and the world was his self-determination to be for
man, and his determining of man to be for himself. "In Jesus Christ
[who is the only form of God's transcendence] God in His free
grace determines Himself for sinful man and sinful man for Himself. He is the election of God before which and without which and
beside which God cannot make any other decision."[115] Because
God is for man and with man, because the world and man are
bracketed by God election, they are given "a simple but comprehensive autonomy."[116]

As the No of crisis turned all the assets of history into liabilities,
now God's Yes erases all liabilities and confronts man with a horizon of permission. The nihilistic tones of Barth's first phase give
place now to "the triumph of grace," in the words of Berkouwer.[117]

But what is the precise meaning of this affirmation that transcendence became time? Does it mean that Barth has now gone a step back and relapsed into the immanentism of the nineteenth century? Does it mean that he is now ready to accept that eternity and time coincide? Does it mean that history becomes now messianic, being thus the bearer of the hope of humanization? No. "What an illusion," says Barth, "to explain it [eternity] as the hidden content of all time, and therefore all time as the vessel—and then only a vessel of eternity."[118] The affirmation that eternity became time is valid only for the time of Jesus Christ and no other time. It is "the time of Jesus Christ [which] is the time of the Lord of time . . . mastered time and for that very reason real, fulfilled time. . . . So the time God has for us . . . is to be regarded as eternal time. . . . The fulfilled time is the time of the years 1–30."[119]

If the fulfilled time, the time which God has for us, is the time of the incarnation, of the historical life of Jesus Christ, what can one say about the time before Christ and the time after him? This question is of basic importance because it has to do with the possibility of humanization in a time that is not the fulfilled time.

Barth answers: "These are different times, distinguished not only by the difference in periods and in contents . . . but distinguished by the varied attitude of God to man."[120]

The time before the fulfilled time is the time of the "unsatisfactory attempt at pedagogy,"[121] a time of "expectation, but *only* of an expectation of the revelation of Jesus Christ,"[122] the time when revelation was "not yet," the time when "the revelation of God will become reality."[123]

The time "after the years 1–30," "like that of prehistory, is quite different from fulfilled time."[124]

The problem becomes more complicated since not all fulfilled time is on the same level. The Easter story is something different, as compared with the years of Jesus' life which preceded it. What is it that makes this time different, the fulfilled time "par excellence"? Barth answers: "Which of the New Testament pronouncements, because they are pronouncements of a definite recollection, are not implicitly or explicitly eschatological?"[125]

The only "big exception"[126] is the time of Easter, which is literally the end of eschatology. The Easter time, says Barth is a "present without any future . . . an eternal presence of God in time. As such it cannot become past, neither needs any future, a time purely present."[127]

The cross is left behind. It is past. The negative intrusion of transcendence into history is no more; it is finished, completed. The old aeon does not exist anymore. It came to an end "with the cross of Christ."[128] There is no place any longer for historical negation. Indeed, "if the old aeon has been done away we do not need to fight against it."[129] The crisis is over.

We remember from our discussion of the political consciousness that the creation of the future is a correlative to the critical negation of the past. Man creates in order to bring the negativity to an end. If, by any chance, the crisis comes to an end (a historical impossibility from the point of view of political humanism) there is no possibility of creating a new future. We could say that if this would ever happen the future would have arrived, would have become present and would be in the process of becoming past. This is precisely the conclusion at which Barth arrives. He declares that although "his [Christ's] resurrection and his parousia are for us two events," this is not the true reality, since for God they are "only one."[130] Actually there is no future as time still open. What seems from the perspective of history to be future is an optical illusion, since for God the two dimensions of time coincide. It is true that Barth admits that Christ is still in motion. "He finds himself in motion or on His way as divine-human mediator, striding from His commencement to the goal already included and indicated in it. . . . As the revealer of His work, He has not yet reached His goal. He is still moving towards it."[131] So it seems that there is an open future after all, a future that remains future even for the Mediator. We should, however, keep in mind that this incompleteness refers to the task of revelation of an already accomplished work. This already accomplished work thus formally and factually determines the limits and the actuality of the future. We should remember that this destruction of the reality of the future is grounded even in Barth's doctrine of the Trinity. Eternity, as the expression of God's being, is "the simultaneity and coincidence of the past, present, and future."[132] If, from the perspective of God, there is no future, how can men behave as though they could create the future? Actually "the time which overarches our time"[133] is the non-eschatological, futureless time, the time which is purely present.

If the humanization of man cannot thus be related to the creation of a new tomorrow, as political humanism thinks, "what does it take to make and to keep human life human in the world?" How to be human if the time of humanization, of transcendence, is already past, and therefore beyond the reach of man's freedom? With existentialism, Barth answers this question by indicating that it is consciousness which transposes man to God's time. It is within the limits of consciousness (obviously determined by the Holy Spirit) that a miracle happens: that which was future ceases to be future, that which was past ceases to be past; they become present. So, expectation and recollection are not forms of absence but modes of contemporaneity. "Where expectation is genuine," comments Barth, " 'previously' does not mean 'not yet'; just as where recollection is genuine, 'subsequently' does not mean 'no longer.' "[134] The problem of humanization is the problem of contemporaneity with the time that God has for us, that is, the time of the coincidence and simultaneity of past, present, and future, the time of resurrection. Indeed, this is the only real time, the time of God for man and therefore the time where man is allowed to be man. "What we mean when we say time," remarks Barth, "is real there. We thus have our time not here but there."[135]

But how does this miracle of transtemporalization occur? The answer to this question is of basic importance, because it is, really, the answer to the question "what does it take to make and to keep human life human in the world?" The answer: Scripture takes us from this time, from our present, it "takes away our time" and transposes us back into the time where we are able to find true liberation.

> It is not therefore an edifying trick of thought, but the assimilation of nourishment absolutely indispensable to our life, when the Holy Scriptures and the proclamation of its message call and transpose us from our time into that time, namely, into the time of Jesus Christ.[136]

> The problem of the Word of God consists in the fact that to this particular man today through the proclamation of this particular Bible text this particular manifestation of God is imparted, that a particular *illic et tunc* becomes a particular *hic et nunc.*[137]

The only humanizing action, the only action that can make possible this miracle of transtemporalization, is thus the preaching of the word, the announcement of the reality of the time which God has for us: the non-eschatological time of the resurrection.

Where is the place for man's work and creativity? In a world where the future is ready, where humanization is a function of preaching, man's action becomes really secondary. It "is not really a creation but a movement within the created world."[138] It is an action that does not negate the given. It rather occurs within the given, as a simple type of movement. The task of humanization becomes thus the monopoly of preachers—ordained or laymen! As to the man who wants to create a new future for man, the man who wants to create history, he is completely mistaken about what he believes to be his vocation. "Even at best, we cannot be more than children engaged in serious and true play."[139]

We come to our conclusion.

Our purpose was to see to what extent Barth's language can help those involved in the task of creating a new future for man. We moved from his first phase, informed by a Kantian-Kierkegaardian concept of transcendence to the second in which God becomes time. What are the conclusions suggested by our dialogue with Barth's theology? We will attempt to summarize them under the three central determinations of the consciousness that looks for a new tomorrow for man.

1. Barth's first phase could have provided great help in the understanding of negation. However, his concept of transcendence made this impossible. God was against the whole world. His transcendence did not insert itself into the world. It could not, as a consequence, allow for the creation of a new tomorrow. It rather brought history to its end.

In his second phase negation is swallowed up by the triumph

of affirmation. The negative does not have real existence. So there is no ground for negative thinking.

2. Negation in his first phase was the counterpart of hope. But because of the against-the-world character of transcendence, hope there referred to a meta-historical reality. It did not allow for concern for the creation of a new tomorrow. There was no room for a historical future.

In the context of the metaphysical triumph of affirmation a similar thing happens: the future becomes past. Real time is not historical time in its unfinished character, but the metaphysical time of resurrection.

3. In both phases humanization is a function of preaching, which is the humanizing task par excellence. Man is not *homo creator*. In the first phase his most creative possibilities are discarded as new forms of rebellion. In the second phase his action is reduced to movement within the given structures. As we reflected about this problem in Barth we recalled what was said against the bureaucrats by a student: "They believe that history has come to an end." Do we not arrive at a similar conclusion here?

It seems that those committed to the creation of a new future, as an exigency of humanization and as the expression of man's transcendence, need to proceed in their search for a language appropriate to their historical project and to their condition as members of the community of faith.

THE LANGUAGE OF THE "THEOLOGY OF HOPE": FROM A PAST THAT IS REJECTED TO A FUTURE THAT IS OFFERED

"What does it take to make and to keep human life human in the world?" Jurgen Moltmann in his *Theology of Hope*[140] suggests, from his dialogue with biblical language, a different paradigm for humanization which we intend to examine now.

His point of departure is the conflict between humanization in terms of being absorbed into timeless eternity, and humanization in terms of participation in a history that moves from a past and a present which are rejected, towards a new future which is offered. Actually he does not start by dealing with humanization except indirectly, by raising the question of revelation. How does biblical language understand the impact of God upon people? What is the nature of this revelation? Moltmann indicates that the influence of Greek methods of thought has led us to think about revelation in terms of that which illuminates "the existing reality of the world or of human nature," that which interprets this reality, "bringing out its truth and using a proper understanding of it to secure man's agreement with it."[141] In the act of revelation man would be confronted with the truth of what is and would thereby become reconciled with it. It would be the "epiphany of the eternal present,"[142] the revelation of the God of Parmenides, the God who eternally is in his perfection, the God who, therefore, in the act of his revelation, liberates man from the transitoriness of history and integrates him into the truth of that which is.

In revelation two basic things would happen: first, man would be confronted with the explanation of the contradictions of the world, from their primordial source; second, man would become integrated into the whole structure of reality. Moltmann remarks, however, that for the Bible, revelation, instead of explaining that which is, "contradicts existing reality" and "thus sets an open stage for history."[143] This is so because for the Bible revelation is not the "epiphany of the eternal present" but rather the revelation of "the God of hope . . . the God with 'future as his essential nature.' "[144] In the first case revelation has to do with "the presence of the eternal." In the second it points to a future promised by the God whose essential nature is the future.[145]

If God is future in his essential nature, we cannot meet him either as an "intra-worldly" or as an "extra-worldly" reality.[146] He cannot be grasped as a "being." He reveals himself as one who is absent, always pointing to the future. His appearance is thus grasped as the uttering of a word of promise. He "encounters us in his promises for the future."[147] We cannot therefore 'have him.' We can "only await in active hope."[148]

If the biblical God is the God who reveals himself in the act of promising a new future for man, we come to a new understanding of humanization in terms of life in response to the hope which the divine promises create. Man is therefore liberated from the limits imposed by the existing structures of the world. He is liberated from the prison of what is and made free to think and behave according to possibilities not immanent in his world. As a matter of fact, "a promise is a declaration which announces the coming of a reality that does not yet exist. . . . The expected future does not have to develop within the framework of the possibilities inherent in the present, but arises from that which is possible to the God of promise."[149] The development of history is not thus to be understood as an immanent process but as the creation of the word. "It is not evolution, progress, and advance that separate time into yesterday and tomorrow, but the word of promise cuts into events and divides reality into one reality which is passing and can be left behind, and another which must be expected and sought."[150] Instead of the future emerging from the untruth of the present, the word of promise "announces the coming of a not yet existing reality from the future of truth."[151]

We are confronted here with an analysis of the consciousness of the community of faith in the Bible which is remarkably close to that of political humanism. As we mentioned before, political humanism is a refusal to admit that history has come to a close (as the "bureaucrats" and the "epiphany of the eternal now" would imply) and the belief that we do not have to think and behave as functions of the given system. On the contrary, man's transcendence is related to his freedom to think and behave in response to a future that does "not yet" exist now except in the form of hope.

But what is the ground for this life in hope? Moltmann answers that "the Christian hope for the future comes of observing a specific, unique event—that of the resurrection and appearing of Jesus Christ."[152] With Barth he affirms that our future depends on an event of the past—the resurrection. Against Barth, however, Moltmann does not identify the event of the resurrection with our future. It is the ground of hope, but the future is not found finished in it. "Christian eschatology" thus "examines the inner tendency of the resurrection event, asking what rightly can and must be expected from the risen and exalted Lord."[153] The resurrection could thus be compared with a seed, with an immanent vitality that has a definite tendency. The basis of the future is already found

hidden in the seed. Likewise, "faith is directed in hope and expecta-
tion towards the revelation of what it has already found hidden in
Christ."[154] But this does not mean that the future has arrived.
Therefore, we have to deal in Christian eschatology with "Jesus
Christ and His future."[155] What is hidden, marches, according to
its inner tendency, to a future which does "not yet" exist.

Christ, thus, is the mirror of our future. Looking towards the
historical horizons they seem closed and blocked. It is when we
turn back and observe a specific event in our past that the future
becomes open. The openness of the future is thus discovered by
reflection.

It is the experience which reflects this event, the hearing of the
word of promise about God's future, which creates history. "The
experience of reality as history was made possible for Israel," Moltmann comments, "by the fact that God was revealed to Israel in his
promises."[156] Because the word of God promises a future beyond
the promises intrinsic in the present, man is set on the move.
History is created. History can thus be described as the creation of
the word that divides history between promise and fulfillment.[157]

But how does this happen?

Moltmann provides a very suggestive answer to this question.

> A promise is a declaration which announces the coming of a
> reality that does not yet exist. Thus promise sets man's heart
> on a future history. . . . The force of promise, and of faith in
> terms of promise, is essentially to keep men on the move in a
> tense *inadequatio rei et intellectus* as long as the *promissio* which
> governs the *intellectus* has not yet found its answer in reality.
> It is from promise that there arises that element of unrest
> which allows of no coming to terms with a present that is
> unfulfilled.[158]

> The remembrance of the promise that has been given . . . bores
> like a thorn in the flesh of every present and opens it for the
> future. In this sense the revelation of the risen Lord does not
> become "historic" as a result of the fact that history continues
> willy-nilly, but it stands as a sort of *primum movens* at the head
> of the process of history. It is in virtue of this revelation that
> the reality of man and his world becomes "historic," and it is
> the hope set upon this revelation that makes all reality inade-
> quate and as such transient and surpassable. It is the *promissio*

inquieta that is the true source of Augustine's *cor inquietum*. It is the *promissio inquieta* that will not suffer man's experience of the world to become a self-contained cosmic image of the deity, but keeps our experience of the world open to history.[159]

The genesis of history can thus be described. Man is immersed in the power of "what is," without any critical distance to negate it, without any future dimension. His consciousness is thus definitely prey to the power of "what is." It is only the word of promise that accordingly creates a new dimension, the *inadequatio rei et intellectus*. Promise is thus the element which, introduced into the intellect, gives it the critical distance to negate "what is." This point must be made clear because it is in sharp opposition to the consciousness of political humanism. For political humanism it is not a promise and a hope from a transcendent realm that make man aware of the pain of his situation. Man is aware of the pain of his situation simply because he is a human being and feels in his flesh the inadequacy between his world and himself and his community. The *inadequatio rei et intellectus* is thus simply a reflection of the inhumanity of the situation. It is from this *inadequatio* that man's consciousness stretches toward the exploration of the unfinished character of his reality, looking for possibilities that will eliminate the negativity of his present. His hope, therefore, is the child of his negation, and totally determined by it. Hope, thus, is historical and related to the form of pain into which man is inserted. For Moltmann, however, the situation is different: there is one transcendental hope (because not related to any specific situation) that makes man aware of the pain of his present. We arrive at the conclusion —very difficult to be substantiated historically—that there is no immediacy between man and the negativity of his present and that he feels this negativity only when it is mediated through a transcendent hope.

The pattern for the historical movement which Moltmann offers is thus basically platonic. It is eros (and not incarnation!) which creates the *cor inquietum*. And more than that: God becomes the *primum movens*, as with Aristotle, pulling history to its future, but without being involved in history.

There cannot be, therefore, any history apart from the con-

sciousness of the Messiah and his hope, apart from the consciousness of the promise. The "passionate suffering and longing" for the
future is only "kindled by the Messiah."[160] It is through the promises that "the hidden future already announces itself and exerts its
influence on the present through the hope it awakens."[161]

The event of promise, therefore, is the beginning of the criticism of everything that is. Because the word of God announces that
the truth is in the future which is promised, the whole present is
negated.

> The expectation of what is to come on the ground of the
> resurrection of Christ must then turn all reality that can be
> experienced and all real experience into an experience that is
> provisional and a reality that does not yet contain within it
> what is held in prospect for it. It must therefore contradict all
> rigid substantio-metaphysical definitions of the common core
> of similarity in world events.[162]
>
> When the world and the human nature bound up with it are
> called into question in this way, then they become "historic,"
> for they are staked upon, and submitted to the crisis of, the
> promised future.[163]

The promised future gives birth to the crisis of the present. It
is not the crisis of the present that gives birth to hope for a promising future. The crisis of the present is thus dependent on the word
which, by giving birth to faith, "measures present reality by the
standard of the word."[164]

The historization of the world is thus an act in which our closed
experience is confronted with the announcing of a different type
of reality which not only contradicts our experience but which
overcomes its negativity. "Present and future," Moltmann remarks, "experience and hope, stand in contradiction to each other
in Christian eschatology . . . , it is the contradiction between the
resurrection and the cross."[165] On the one hand the present and its
negativity; on the other hand the future where God reveals his
faithfulness, the world that stands at the end of God's promise.
Moltmann explains the contents of the contradiction of the Christian experience, mother of the *inadequatio rei et intellectus,* by
quoting Calvin: "To us is given the promise of eternal life—but to

us, the dead. A blessed resurrection is proclaimed to us—meantime we are surrounded by decay. We are called righteous—and yet sin lives in us."[166]

The cross, as the expression of the present, as that which expresses the content of our human experience, stands for a life with all future possibilities blocked, a life in which every value is reduced to nothing by the power of finitude and decay. So it was with Jesus. His cross, says Moltmann, "implies not only the end of the life which he had, but also the end of the life which he loves and in which he hopes."[167] The cross stands, thus, for death, for the end, for a situation with no possibilities whatsoever, for the end of the future and the end of hope. It stands for our present experience which is void of transcendence, since God is pure futurity. There is thus a "gap" between cross and resurrection that can be traversed only by an act of "creatio ex nihilo,"[168] an act, however, that never becomes history, and that is made present to us only in the form of promise. Indeed, "the revelation of the risen Lord does not become 'historic' as a result of the fact that history continues willy-nilly, but it stands as a sort of *primum movens* at the head of the process of history."[169] It is not historical, but "pulls" history. It is qualitatively "wholly other," as in Barth. In terms of relation it is tangential, as in Barth. The impact of its announcement is the advent of "crisis," as in Barth. Its promise is a new world that comes when all human possibilities are ended, as in Barth. Moltmann's position suggests itself compellingly to me as a 90-degree rotation of the idea of transcendence of the early Barth. The "infinite qualitative difference between time and eternity" stands for the *ex nihilo* gap that separates us from the future of God, always elusive, always ahead, never present, never history, always act, never being, only apprehended in the proclamation of the word.

The consequence of this position is going to be of crucial importance for a possible dialogue with political humanism. In our analysis of political humanism we indicated that hope is born from negation. Negation, thus, as a part of the human experience of man in history, is an expression of transcendence and mother of man's futurity. We are dealing here with transcendence in the midst of life, transcendence revealed as the negation of negativity. It is from man's participation in the negation of history that there emerges a new possibility for a new future, out of the concrete, incarnated situation of pain into which man is inserted. The negation of the facts on the part of this consciousness "does not come from its perception of a pattern prior to the perception of the facts, and for this reason eternal, but rather from its disagreement with the pattern of the future extracted from its perception of the present reality. . . . The plan is induced from reality, it is empirical, which is the basis for its effectiveness."[170] The negation of pain is thus the mother of hope and effectiveness. The cross, suffering, is therefore an integral part of the dialectical thrust that moves in the direction of a new future for man. It is not only the source of the stretching of the consciousness in the search for the arrested possibilities of the situation, but it determines the shape of hope, since hope exists for the sake of the man who suffers. "It is only for the sake of those without hope that hope is given to us."[171]

In Moltmann, however, the process takes a totally different shape. Hope cannot emerge from our experience, from our present, from the cross. It comes "from a future of truth." The future is not created out of the negation, but on the contrary, it is this transcendental future which negates what is. This future is transcendental because it claims to be "a pattern prior to the perception of the facts, and for this reason eternal." It is a future that claims to reconcile the contradictions of the present experience. "The future of the resurrection," Moltmann comments, "comes to it as it takes upon itself the cross: Thus the eschatology of the future and the theology of the cross are interwoven."[172] I find it difficult to see where they are interwoven, although it is obvious that they are related in terms of negation and fulfillment: resurrection negates the reality of the cross and creates a new world of fulfillment, *ex nihilo.* It is difficult to see where they are interwoven because if God is the God who is essentially future, therefore totally tangential to the present, how is this relation possible? The relationship which is obvious is that the transcendental world of resurrection promises to overcome the "closeness" of the world of experience, of cross, of death. Cross and resurrection, however, are not seen as two dialectical poles of transcendence, as it creates a new tomorrow for man. And when this happens an absolutely fundamental element is lost in the understanding of "what it takes to make and to keep human life human in the world": the basically political character of history.

It seems to me that this is evident in Moltmann's exposition. Let us consider first his understanding of the cross: the categories he uses to describe it are basically organic, related to decay, finitude, and death, coming close to what Teilhard de Chardin calls the "passivities of diminishment." The import of the resurrection for such an understanding of the "negativity" of our experience is that "through the knowledge of the resurrection of the crucified the contradiction is always and everywhere perceptible in an unredeemed world, and the sorrow and suffering caused by that world are taken up into the confidence of hope."[173] The impact upon consciousness then is to the effect that now, instead of seeing the world as closed by death, it takes it as open.

> Hope does not take things as they happen to stand or lie, but as progressing, moving things with possibilities of change.[174] Resurrection, as the ultimate reality, as the *primum movens* which pulls history, informs consciousness that actually the world is open, progressing. Hope and anticipation of the future as a consequence . . . are realistic ways of perceiving the scope of our real possibilities, and as such they set everything in motion and keep it in a state of change.[175]

The conclusion at which we arrive is this: the promise of the resurrection, as the result of the *creatio ex nihilo*, in absolute discontinuity with history, informs us about the openness of the process in which we are, where everything is progressing. The discontinuity between future and present informs us about the continuous process by which the present moves towards the future, in spite of that which seems to interrupt that progressive movement, namely, decay and death. The result of this position is very strange. We remember Marcuse's criticism of the technological society in its ability to make man think functionally, within the limits of the possible, dictated by the system. This way of thinking would presuppose that the human future is in continuity with the given system, seminally present in it. He indicated how this world became closed, thus eliminating the negative ways of thinking. In this context, it is only when man comes to realize the closedness of the world in which he lives that he arrives at the position where he is able to negate it. The realization of the closing power of the given world is thus the prerequisite for the kind of action which makes it open. On the contrary, Moltmann declares:

> . . . the transforming mission requires in practice a certain *Weltanschauung*, a confidence in the world and a hope for the world. It seeks for that which is really, objectively possible in this world, in order to grasp it and realize it in the direction of the promised future of righteousness . . . Hence it regards the world as an open process.[176]

The *Weltanschauung* informed by hope sees the world as an open process. The given, therefore, is a process open to the future possibilities of righteousness. Once again Moltmann approaches Barth: the old aeon is destroyed; we no longer have to fight against it. The closed world is a past, already overcome possibility. For hope, cross and death are left behind. They do not belong to the reality which pulls history.

This conclusion, however, basically contradicts the experiences that gave birth to political humanism.

First, history is not open. The problem of future and hope in history is not related primarily to decay and death but to the powers that keep history captive. The cross does not stand for dying, but for killing, for the powers that destroy men. History is thus not closed by organic realities but by active powers of political nature. The cross is thus never a reality left behind, eliminated by hope.

Second, we cannot assume, therefore, that history is progressing, moving towards new possibilities. History is to be made open. And this means a confrontation with the powers that keep it captive. Resurrection, thus, never exists without the cross, without the confrontation. It does not exist transcendentally, but it comes into being when freedom goes through conflict with the powers that make history captive.

Third, history is set on the move not by a *primum movens* but rather by the dialectic of freedom, as it is incarnated in the world's sufferings, and which, as a consequence, gives birth to negation, hope, and action. The structure of transcendence is thus always dialectical and historical, and never undialectically and ahistorically related to a transcendent hope. In short: political humanism does not operate with categories borrowed from the organic realm, as Moltmann usually does, when he interprets cross and resurrection. For instance, to relate cross and resurrection as latency to tendency seems very close to Aristotle's interpretation of organic movement: in the seed we find the form in a latent state, whereas in the fully developed plant, the actualized form, we find the natural tendency of the movement.

For political humanism, both negation and hope are permanent determinations of transcendence in the creation of a new tomorrow for man. The elimination of one of the poles for the sake of the other is, *ipso facto*, suicide, the destruction of hope and consequently the abortion of the new tomorrow.

Moltmann's last words in his book have to do with the mission of the Church. If the Church has its being in its faith in the proclamation of the future of Jesus Christ, as the future which proclaims the openness of history, its intelligence is turned towards "the theoretical and practical recognition of the structure of historic process and development inherent in the situation requiring to be ordered, and thus of the potentialities and the future of that situation."[177] This means that to the Church is given the apostolate of hope that involves the world of nations in the exodus from the present of a self-contained existence into the promised future. "This hope," Moltmann remarks, "makes the Church the source of continuous new impulses towards the realization of righteousness, freedom, and humanity."[178]

The climax of Moltmann's theology is not simply that the Church is called to work for justice in the world. What he really says is that history is a mode of human experience which is not accessible to the world save through the Church. It is the word of promise that creates the *cor inquietum*, the *inadequatio rei et intellectus*. Where the word of promise is not announced there is no hope and consequently no history. The Church, accordingly, has a historizing function in the world.

At the end Moltmann comes close to Bultmann and Barth:

what makes human life human in the world, namely, transcendence, is mediated by an act of consciousness as it looks back to a
certain event of the past. The only mode of God's presence in the
world would be the word of promise, the word that points to his
elusiveness, to his future.

In the last instance the action which genuinely relates man to
transcendence is the preaching and the hearing of the word. The
effect of this position upon action follows naturally: action is not
born out of the exigency of the situation; action is not the creative
act that historizes man's negation and hope; action becomes imitation. Man, therefore, is not the creator of the new future. He is
rather the one who acts "in the light of the promised future that is
to come."[179] Moltmann even refers to "the things that constitute
the history which 'corresponds' to this kind of revelation."[180] It is
action that expresses obedience to a future but does not create that
future. This concept of "action which corresponds to" the future
presented by revelation is very problematical. It seems to me that
the only political attitude that would really "correspond" to the
future would be pacifism. How to make room for conflict, struggle,
if our action is to "correspond" to the future which revelation
brings to us? This problem is related to the elimination of dialectics
in God, on the part of Moltmann, by the overcoming of the cross
towards a total concentration on the *primum movens* which pulls
history.

The main objection to Moltmann's conclusion, however, is
simply that it is not true that the Church has been the midwife of
the future. Moreover, it is not true that where the word is not
preached there is no history. Indeed, our historical experience today is exactly the opposite. Many of the movements that today
display the deepest concern for the creation of a new tomorrow for
man, and that have taken the greatest risks this adventure presents,
operate within the limits of a purely secular and humanist assessment of the situation. How is it possible to make room for the
secular movements committed to the task of creating a new future
for man if it is only the faithful hearing of the word of promise that
historizes man? How can this question be answered in a world
becoming more and more secularized? How to tell Christians,

engaged with secular man, atheists, in the task of creating a new tomorrow for mankind, that all these men are not really historical? Could we say that—since their hope is born out of their suffering, and not out of the hearing of the word, as Moltmann suggests— they are not historical? Can we say that only those who hear the word have hope? The result of Moltmann's theology would be the profanization of the secular,[181] exactly as we find in Bultmann and in the early Barth. Secularization would thus be the same as dehis- torization. And historization would be dependent on the world's attention to the word of the Church. For those who are opting for positions that operate within a secular framework, Moltmann's theology remains as a very problematic point of reference, since his tangential concept of transcendence, the source of historization, is mediated only by the word through the Church.

We could summarize the conflict between Moltmann's para- digm and that of political humanism in this way:

1. Political humanism affirms that the human consciousness, from its position of with-ness, of incarnation in, insertion into the negative of what is, is able to negate the inhuman of "what is." The transcendent in man is thus deeply rooted in his present, since it is the source of the negation.

For Moltmann there is no transcendent in the present. There- fore, it is impossible for the secular man to negate from the im- mediacy of his suffering. "What is" is therefore all powerful over man. This consciousness remains profane.

2. Political humanism understands hope as the stretching out of human consciousness, as it looks beyond the unfinishedness of "what is." The time of the future, thus, grows out of transcendence informed by suffering. It is the painful present that projects itself in the direction of a hopeful future. In theological language: the resurrection is the child of the cross.

Moltmann, however, does not start from the negation of the present but from the transcendental promise. The transcendental promise is the source of eros which sets history on the move. In theological language: it is not the incarnation which is the mother of the future, but rather the transcendental future which makes man aware of the incarnation. It is the transcendental future that makes man aware of the dimensions of suffering which his historical situation contains. The incarnation remains thus profane in itself because it only contains the possibility of "end," "decay," "death." It is only from the other side that the future becomes open. Obviously no room is made for the coincidence of transcendence and secular. The influence of platonism and the danger of docetism are obvious.

3. Political humanism sees the future as a horizon of possibilities, open, to be filled by the creation of freedom mediated to history by action. Man thus creates the future, which is never determined. This is why action is so important for humanization, because there is nothing awaiting man that does not bear the mark of his action. Moltmann, however, sees the future as already determined. True, it is not ready, but it is, nevertheless already determined. It is this future which attracts man by eros: the future is an object and not a horizon. Because the future stands as the *primum movens* to history, human action is not creation but a "movement" (Barth) which reflects the object of hope.[182]

The basic conflict between the language of political humanism and the language of hope suggested by Moltmann is that the former understands negation, hope, and the creation of the new future as starting basically from the condition of man in his insertion into history, his "incarnation." The latter, on the contrary, sees this situation as profane, without possibilities. The only possibility becomes real when man is confronted with a non-historical and transcendent reality that does not have any dimension in the present, being only mediated by the word. The conflict is between those, on the one hand, who have accepted the secular as their frame of reference and "who do not first seek behind the stars for a reason to go under and be a sacrifice, but who sacrifice themselves for the earth," and on the other hand, those who become historical only when they look behind the stars and are then set in motion by eros.

Toward a New Language

Christians committed to the historical liberation of man have, for a long time, been aware of the conflict between their ultimate concern and the language which they used to speak. They have discovered that their language, instead of creating "new possibilities of addressing and understanding the reality which approaches them,"[183] has been remarkable for its paralyzing effect. Ebeling observes that languages are expression of a certain spirit. It is the spirit that distinguishes one language from another. This means that in order to be truthfully spoken,[184] the spirit of the language must be expressive of the spirit of the man who speaks it. The experience of these Christians has been just the opposite. They find themselves caught by the contradiction between, on the one hand, the spirit of the language of faith they were taught to speak, and, on the other, their own spirit, dominated by the vision of and passion for human liberation. It is true that this language claims to be the language of freedom, liberation, and life. The words which its universe of discourse contains are very eloquent in this regard. However, "we do not get at the nature of words by asking what they contain, but by asking what they effect, what they set going, what future they disclose."[185] It is at this point that it has become obvious for many that it is no longer possible to speak truthfully the language they once learned. The situation is a veritable moment of truth. It raises the question of self-identity, of authenticity. Who am I? Am I the one who is ultimately concerned for the creation of a new tomorrow, or the one who repeats the words once learned? Where is my "spirit"? For many Christians the conflict between the spirit of the language and the spirit of their commitment does not seem to offer a serious problem. They learned how to live at the same time in two different and opposing worlds without being thereby torn apart. Others, however, cannot live in a divided world, and have necessarily to look for a language which is expressive of the purity of heart of which Kierkegaard spoke, the purity of heart which exists only when there is integrity and unity, when man wills one thing only. For the sake of this purity of heart a large number of Christians have decided to unlearn the language they were once taught. They arrived at the conclusion that faith cannot become a language expressive of their passion for human liberation. How could they be free for the task of creating a new future for man if the language of faith did not make room for this freedom?

How could they be totally committed to this passion, as a flame which burns for the sake of one thing only, if their old language was spoken by a different "spirit"?

Other Christians, however, have stubbornly refused to forget the language of faith. The reason for this refusal is that in the very moment of the death of the old language they discovered that, hidden under what was frozen and paralyzing in it, there was a spirit very similar to their own. The death of the old language, accordingly, was the end of what was repressive of its liberating, future-oriented thrust. The event of death becomes thus the occasion for resurrection, since a new language has begun to take shape.

We remarked earlier that a language, since it is expressive of a spirit, marks the limits of a community. The creation of a new language, in its turn, implies the death of a certain spirit and the triumph of a new one. This means, necessarily, the creation of a new community. If one abandons a language which expressed a certain spirit that moved a community, one's new spirit and new community are necessarily separated from the old ones. It cannot be denied that there is a certain discontinuity which separates them. But if this is the case, how can one still claim to belong to the community of faith and to speak the language of faith? Are not the new language and new community something totally different, totally new? In order to answer this question we have to remember that the community of faith is a community of men who live in history, amid other human communities. It speaks with the voice of men and not from a meta-historical point of reference. This means that its language is always an expression of its historical and therefore relative position. Consequently, as its locus in history changes, new problems arise, new tasks are presented, new languages are spoken in the world, so the language of the community of faith moves, responds, and changes. Its voice should have the freshness and relativity of all historical subjects.

Does this mean that the language of faith is simply an echo of its environment? Is it the language of adaptation? If this is the case, to what degree are we justified in calling it the language of faith? Does not faith provide for its language an eternal point of reference that enjoys the stability of a rock amid historical relativity? There has been a strong tradition in the history of the Church that has interpreted faith in these terms. Faith makes man free from history as it takes him away from history. Its language is thus to be expressive of an island of stability and meaning amid the ever changing sphere of time and space. Faith is considered to be a "turning away from the restlessness and busyness of the world and a turning towards the stillness and peace of the divine."[186]

There are elements in the consciousness of the community of faith, however, which suggest that it is not only possible but indeed necessary to understand faith in exactly the opposite sense, as a radically historical mode of being, as "the acceptance of truly historical existence."[187] If this is the case, its language consequently must express the spirit of freedom for history, of taste for the future, of openness for the provisional and relative. The language of the community of faith therefore, cannot be stabilized. If the spirit of faith is permanent openness toward history, its language must be continuously going through a process of death and resurrection, as it leaves the old and moves toward the new. When the language of faith, for its own preservation, refuses to die and remains as the repetition of a language of the past, it ceases to be historical. As such it is like the presence of a frozen corpse, the presence of what once was alive but now, after death, still remains in the world of the living. As such it is not simply frozen—it also freezes as well: it refuses to allow the new to come to life.

The life of the language of faith, therefore, depends on its ability to negate itself, to change, to die in order to gain a new life.

How does this process of death and resurrection occur? Karl Barth and later Paul Lehmann suggested that the language of the community of faith must be understood as occurring between the reading of the Bible and the reading of newspapers.[188] It is, therefore, neither a simple description of a past that fills the screen of memory nor a description of the present now confronting man. It rather expresses a dialectical relationship between the two. On the one hand the present forces the past to remain open. The community brings to its act of remembering its experience of the sufferings and joys of the present, of its negativity and possibilities. The past is never allowed to become a screen because the community that remembers cannot deny the present in which it lives. On the other hand, the past forces the present to remain open. The past is like a horizon where the signs of dawn begin to appear for the man who is amid the darkness of the suffering and hopelessness of his present. Through the promise which the past presents, man is made free to think about the possibility of a new tomorrow. The act of remembering is thus, as an expression of love for the present —and only as such—a liberating possibility. It provides new grounds for negation, new possibilities of hope, new freedom for action. It is this dialectical relationship that keeps the language of faith always in permanent movement. It could not be otherwise, because its present is historical and never comes to a halt. And it is thanks to this fluidity that this language is able to express the vitality of a community whose spirit is directed towards the future.

The history of the community of faith could be written as the history of the birth, death, and resurrection of its languages. Old languages die when they remain frozen as the world moves ahead. When this happens, they cease to be instruments of liberation and become structures of repression. The new is aborted for the sake of the old. However, when the community begins to feel again the pains and challenges of the present, its act of remembering creates a new freedom both to unlearn the old language and to create a new one. The language of freedom for the life of justification by faith was created somehow according to this pattern. Luther was tormented by fear and anxiety before the awareness of man's impotence to find grounds of liberation within himself. How to achieve liberation from fear? Is it possible for man's subjectivity to be expressive of abandonment instead of statistical calculation about his power of performance? Within the universe of discourse of the language of the Church all exits seemed blocked. From this situation of suffering the act of remembering—his rediscovery of Paul —acquired a liberating import. Memory became the flame which thawed the frozen language that was keeping man under bondage, thereby making possible the creation of a new language which expressed both man's freedom from fear and for life. A similar process is behind the theological language of existentialism. The thorn of the present was and is both the threat of man being lost within the massive structures of the world and the profanization of the world by scientific reason. It was as an answer to this situation that memory made possible the creation of a language expressive of man's freedom in spite of the closed character of the objective horizons of history.

For Barth the problem of the inadequacy of the prevailing language of faith was a different one. He contemplated the end of the optimistic hopes of the nineteenth century with World War I and the radical question mark which this event put before and after all the languages that took for granted man's power to liberate history from its contradictions. From this critical historical present, Barth was able to rediscover the negative and critical words of the universe of discourse of the Bible. Teilhard de Chardin in turn was dominated by a profound sense of tragedy created by the same war, coupled with both a deep existential anxiety before finitude and a personal commitment to the world of science. Before these problems the prevailing language of his community of faith remained mute, unable to open the way toward the future. The dialogue between his present and the horizons of the past became then the occasion for the creation of a new language in which both the past was brought to life again and the present was set into a new context of confidence. These cases, selected at random, show how there are situations in which the problems of the present cannot be solved if the old language is not forgotten and a new one is created. This event of discontinuity, instead of being the end of faith, is rather the only means whereby it is kept alive.

This analysis clarifies the task that Christians committed to the historical liberation of man have ahead of themselves: the creation of a new language expressive of their "ultimate concern" and at the service of its fulfillment. Three things must be remembered.

1. This task is understood only by the community of faith as it discovers itself ultimately concerned for the creation of a new tomorrow for man.

2. The community of faith must take the criticism of political humanism and bring it to bear upon its own language. Only thus will those aspects opposed to the "spirit" expressive of passion for and vision of human liberation be unmasked as such.

3. The new language must add something to what is promised by the language of political humanism. Otherwise, it is superfluous and cannot claim to be a genuine expression of the spirit of the community of faith. It would be simply an echo of political humanism, a reduplication of an already existing language, its translation into religious jargon. This means that the new language is to be judged by (a) its power to criticize even the language that, in the first moment of the process, negated the language of the community of faith; (b) its power to offer greater and wider horizons for hope; and finally (c) the freedom it provides for human activity. The method is not artificially imposed. It simply follows the dialectic of the life of the Christian community in its search for a language expressive of its commitment to the liberation of man.

CHAPTER TWO

THE VOCATION FOR FREEDOM

Our analysis of the language of political humanism indicated that the consciousness which speaks it is determined by a vocation for freedom. Its negation of the inhuman in the present, its openness to hope, its concern for the transformation of negation and hope into history through political action, are the signs that lead us to describe it as a consciousness determined by freedom and committed to the task of human liberation.

How may we account for this vocation for freedom? Why refuse when everybody says adapt? Why negate when everybody affirms? Why be free for the future when everybody is domesticated by the present? The vocation for freedom is a reality that refuses to be accounted for. It stands as a protest, as a contradiction, in discontinuity with the world in which it lives. It is this element, this vocation for freedom, that has led many Christians to discover themselves as a part of the community of those who are committed to the task of human liberation. Because the most fundamental element of the consciousness of the community of faith is a similar vocation for freedom. As Paul Lehmann points out, they find themselves united in the same "passion for and vision of human deliverance."[1] They are discovering that their eyes are turned toward a common future and their hands committed to the same task. Although their languages are very often conflicting, the fact is that the conflicts do not eliminate a common ground for dialogue, since their common involvement in the task of liberation and their common vocation for freedom provide a historical context in which an ongoing, critical conversation, for the sake of their hopes and tasks, is made both possible and necessary. One could very well remind the theologian that the language of faith has not been exemplary in its concern for the historical liberation of man, nor has the community of faith been outstanding in its commitment to the creation of a new tomorrow. Indeed, the previous critique of the language of some theological paradigms was intended precisely to make the community of faith aware of the apolitical, ahistorical and even conservative tones of its language. What is interesting, however, is that in spite of this fact Christians are, historically, becoming more and more committed to the task of human liberation. And when they do this they are simply recovering an element which is absolutely central, although many times forgotten, in the consciousness of the community of faith, namely, its vocation to freedom.

When Christians discover themselves as the rebels, as a part of the "Great Refusal," as those who cannot adapt, as the disturbers of the prevailing order, they are not, therefore, betraying a tradition of conformism and passivity but rather recovering what is most fundamental and primordial in the history and consciousness of the community of faith. As a matter of fact, the most primitive fragments of its memory already express the reality of the vocation for freedom. The community of faith understood that it lived in a world of expanding horizons, always being made open to possibilities nonexistent before. Human life was thus seen as a happening in history, in a time which was open-ended in the direction of the future. As we remarked before, there is nothing that can explain the why of this vocation. G. E. Wright observes: "We can never be certain of the true reason for this particular Israelite view of nature and history. It is the primary, irreducible datum of Biblical theology, without antecedents in the environment whence it might have evolved."[2] This vocation for freedom stood in sharp opposition to all the then prevalent models of human life and society which were shaped according to the pattern of nature and cyclical time and which, consequently, understood human life in terms of adaptation to the given, natural structures of life.

It is because of this vocation for the future and history that the Old Testament is, to a great degree, the history of a permanent conflict between the community of faith, and the paradigms for humanization that implied the de-futurization of man.

The violent opposition to the worship of Baal is one of these cases. The fact that this worship was of a sexual nature, used sexual symbols, and required the sexual act as part of its ritual could mislead us in the understanding of the significance of the conflict. Was it a reaction against sexual immorality? For the worshipers of Baal sex was not immoral but divine. It was the source of life and the power that made humanization possible. They received their lives as a permanent gift of the fields which yielded their fruit and were always dependent on the repetition of the miracle of the rebirth of nature after its death. How could they avoid a sense of wonder and gratitude before the hidden sources of fertility and life? The reason why nature was so miraculous, always increasing the sources of life, it was thought, was that it was sexual in character. "Apparently it is in the depth of the ground that the cause of this increase lies hid. For there . . . male and female powers, Baal and Baalath, 'lord' and 'lady' copulate, countless pairs of deities."[3] The sexual nature of the Baal worship was not, therefore, anything immoral, according to its presuppositions. Was not nature, the giver of life, sexual in its inner structure? The sexual act was thus, "an act of sacral pairing, in which man and woman imitate the deities, identifying them with themselves, so to speak." They can thus "enhance the force and working of the divine fecundity."[4]

Baal expresses in this way "the all-embracing harmony of the universe, . . . the primal and the ultimate identity of all that is, the unity of all the elements of life, human, superhuman, and subhuman, in a single and comprehensive totality."[5] It is because there is an "all embracing harmony" in which all the expressions of life are united in a single totality that man is able to activate fertility by imitation. Imitation has the effect of accelerating the inner productive possibilities already given in the system of nature. The act of worship was, thus, one in which man affirmed and reenacted his solidarity with the totality by making his action an imitation of the pattern offered by organism. The sexual act was the technique to ensure the proper functioning of the system, without surprises, interruptions, or novelties. In this action, therefore, man did not create anything new. It was simply a movement within the world, a technical handling of the given. What did he expect from his tomorrow? That nature would not be disturbed by anything unexpected but rather that its fertility would work itself out normally and abundantly. "Man's security was found in the way he fitted himself into this divine harmony," observes Wright. "Man's greatest good was to be caught up within this cosmic rhythm of nature."[6]

Humanization, consequently, is the result of man's harmony with the system of nature which contains him and of which he is a part. What is the greatest danger? The new, the unexpected. These are the elements that break the harmony and therefore interrupt the normal cycle of life, in its return to its first beginning and primordial harmony. Whereas the community of faith looked for a new tomorrow and lived like a wanderer, always expecting and longing for the unexpected, the worshiper of nature accepted as his vocation to be domesticated by the natural processes. He lived therefore in a world

> . . . in which the emphasis is upon order, harmony, and integration. The worlds of society, nature, and the gods interpenetrate in such a way that the *status quo* is the focus of attention. [Consequently] all polytheisms tend to be religions of the *status quo* and none of them has ever produced a thoroughly social revolution. . . . Revolution of any sort is abhorrent to the inmost nature of such natural religion.[7]

This conclusion is necessary: if man's life was a gift of the system of nature, if nature was the mother from whose womb man had come, from whose breasts he received nourishment, and to whose womb he would return again, his security depended on the mother's stability which, in its turn, demanded conformity on the part of the son.

Van Leeuwen calls our attention to another "refusal" in the tradition of the community of faith, in which its vocation for the future expresses itself again. This refusal is found in the story of the end of the Tower of Babel. Van Leeuwen comments:

> The Old Testament is to be read as a unique account or documentation of the people of Israel's struggle to preserve their peculiar genius by breaking away from the pattern of a pri-

mary civilization. The story of the tower of Babel reflects the radical judgment of Israel's faith upon a conception of totality basic to the Babylonian religion and society.[8]

The story tells about the failure of man's endeavors to build "a city and a tower with its top in the heavens" (Gen 11:4). It is told that this decision was made because men were afraid of the future. The tower was to bring integration, unity, and stability. It stands for a world view familiar to the Babylonians of antiquity, in which the universe was seen as an integrated totality. Their temple-towers —the "ziggurat," referred to in the biblical story as the tower of Babel—were structures that represented this totality: the waters, the earth, the heavens and stars, men and gods, everything was united in a harmonious whole. The society of men was thus to be an expression of the universe, and only when it functioned as an integrated part of the whole did man find his own integration and harmony with the whole. The temple as the center and highest expression of the society of men—indeed, the expression of their joint activity—was believed to be like "the string which binds heaven and earth together."[9] The society of man was thus an integral part of the society of the gods. It was ontocratic in character, grounded on and structured according to the totality that embraced it. It was not historical, provisional, marching towards a new tomorrow. Since it was a link in the structure of being in the universe, the actions of men were, as happened with the Baal worship, intended to produce stability and to imitate the all-embracing order. The movement of the stars is the order that determines the rhythm of the actions of men. This is why the science of astronomy in its origins was wholly subordinated to the purpose of determining the timing of the society of men. Consequently the time of men was not horizontal but cyclical. Horizontal time, time that moved toward the new, time that was not synchronized with the system of nature, was time of disorder and disintegration, time in which man was uprooted from the whole, time in which man lost his grasp over his future, time which was headed toward chaos and destruction.

The logic of this paradigm is both precise and attractive. It can be understood in two tempos. The first tempo is scientific observation and mathematical description of what is. This observation and description provided the elucidation of the context and limits of man. What is the great sin? To stand critically over against the given. The given order and given structures are expressions of the truth of what is. The logic moves then smoothly to the second tempo: man bows to the power of the truth of what is. He renounces negation and creation. Indeed, there is no room for these categories inside this system. His actions and thought become functional. His thought is to describe what is. He cannot explore possibilities because they simply do not exist. His actions are movements in harmony with the totality. The goal of his life: to adapt, to fit in.

The biblical story transforms this paradigm into a joke. The seriousness of men, their pretension to live without cutting the umbilical cord that links heaven and earth, their "scientific" paradigm for humanization, end up in confusion. Men are scattered all over the earth and forced to live at a much more modest level. The failure of the enterprise does not remain, in the biblical story, a regrettable failure. It is a failure that is welcomed, is indeed even necessary, because it makes possible the option that determined Israel's consciousness, the option for history. "The refashioning of the tower of Babel story," observes van Leeuwen, "is part of the fatal attack" which the Bible "launches against precisely that conception of totality for which the ziggurat . . . stands."[10] This attack, however, has meaning only when seen as the negative side of the consciousness of a community which had opted for history. With the protest that Israel raises "against the religion of cosmic totality, against the 'sacralizing' of all being, against the supremacy of fate, against the divinizing of kings and kingdoms" . . . "history is discovered. . . . Here there is proper room for man and here the taste of freedom. The world is now radically secularized, . . . moving forward . . . [and becomes, therefore] the arena of history."[11]

In the New Testament the same polemics take on another form in the radical rejection of law as a paradigm for humanization. "No human being," Paul affirms, "will be justified . . . by the works of the law" (Rom 3:20). Law appears here to be related to everything which is anti-man. It is the source of fear. Obedience to it gives birth to boasting. Life under law is slavery. Ultimately it is the power which ministers death![12] Why, in the New Testament, is law, which was accepted as having been given by God, which belonged to the memory of the community, now under attack? It seems that for the New Testament writers law suffered a historical perversion. In the words of Paul, the intention of the command-ment was life (Rom 7:10) but man did not discover life in it. It became rather the source of fear, bondage, and death. Jesus pointed out the same problem when he indicated that the original meaning of the commandment was that it was for the sake of man,[13] whereas now it had gone through a freezing process that made of it an antihuman power: it was man who was for the sake of the com-mandment. It was true that the commandment had been given by God. It had been given, however, on the way from a past of bond-age to a new tomorrow, on the way from Egypt to the promised land. It had been given as the discipline of historical life, for the sake of the new tomorrow which had to be created. The law was thus related to a primordial experience of the community that was in radical opposition to the options for adaptation and conformity to the status quo. On the contrary, the law should be regarded as a sort of preparation for the new toward which the community was mov-ing. Now, however, the law had suffered a dehistorizing transposi-tion, and came to mean "the totality of the historically given legal demands."[14] It was the presence of the past that became frozen and now claimed to be the determining factor of man's behavior. This process of dehistorization of the law and its consequent dehistoriz-ing power became very clear as it related to the issue of the "sab-bath." In the historical experience of the community, the sabbath was a day of rest "on the way toward" a new tomorrow. It was a pause not in the routine of cyclical time but rather a moment of relaxation on the way toward a new day. It is not our purpose to explore its meaning here but rather to indicate the totally historical character in which it was originally set. It was a pause in the movement toward the new. Its dehistorization, however, robbed it of this dimension, destroyed its character of pause in the expecta-tion of the creation of the new. The time of the sabbath became similar to the cyclical time of the religions of nature: man had to adapt, to fit in, to be in harmony with, and to abdicate the creation of anything new. The sabbath was the time of the old. Every succeeding sabbath would be a repetition of what had already oc-

curred. Any human event that demanded an unusual type of action
—such as the healing of the sick—was an abnormality that had to
be left untouched. The liberating day became the petrifying one.
What is true for the sabbath is true for the whole law. It was
dehistorized and transformed into an abstract command of the
divine, an ahistorical expression of what was eternally true, a set of
moral values given to man in the "epiphany of the eternal present."[15] The paradigm for humanization ceased to be an expectation
of the new and became conformity to the old.

The meaning of the conflict between Gospel and law is of
ultimate importance because it seems that there is no single concept
that had a greater influence upon Western philosophical and theological ethics than that of law. First of all it was Platonism which
suggested that the human "polis" was to be built in accordance with
the eternal world of ideas. Worshipers of Baal, the scientists of the
motion of the stars, and the Greek philosophers had a common
conviction: the city of man, in order to be the locus of humanization, had to be built as a part of and according to the whole. It is
true that their models were widely different and even opposed. All
of them agreed, however, that "the epiphany of the eternal present" offered the elements for the building of the social order. A city
built upon what was accidental, historical, not according to the
eternal, could not avoid the tragedy of disintegration. What is the
ground for the Greek "polis"? What is the source of its laws? The
eternal order or simply the contingencies of history? This is the
drama that Sophocles describes in his *Antigone.* Moreover, Stoicism
added its contribution along the same line, with its idea of *lex
naturae*, the law intrinsic to the nature of things. The influence of
law upon Christian thought was so pervasive that even God came
to be seen as essentially law; grace came to be considered as an a
posteriori arrangement on the part of God in order to make possible
for man either to be righteous before God's law (Roman Catholic
theology) or to be considered as righteous, on account of Christ's
merits, before God's tribunal (Calvin). Grace is here what makes
the fulfillment of law possible. The paradigm of order triumphs
since grace is seen as extra power provided for man, in order to
make possible his adaptation to the given structures of eternal val-

ues. In the words of Catholic theology, grace heals nature. We would be tempted to say that there is a radical interruption, a wide gulf between the ethics of the worship of sexuality or of the Babylonian world view, on the one hand, and the values created by the idea of law in Christian thought, on the other, and that we should therefore differentiate between them. This is true. Our purpose, however, is not to make a comparison of values but rather to indicate that when human behavior and society are dominated by the concept of law and legality, as expressions of an eternal order of values, man's historicity is destroyed. Man is human to the extent to which he adapts to and fits into an ahistorical, eternal idea of man and society. Action becomes imitation. Man does not march toward a new tomorrow, since law and legality, as already given in the past, become the model of his action in the future.

When nature or any sort of order becomes the context which man elects for his life, history comes to an end. At least man loses his openness towards the future since the future is to be the imitation of the values once given in the past.

It is precisely against this good that man can perform by imitation, against his pretension to conform to a world of eternal values, that the New Testament directs its protest. It understands that man's efforts to fulfill the law are expressions of his unfreedom, his fear of the future, his lack of confidence in God. Man's success in performing the good and man's slavery and fear go together, forming one single cluster. As Bultmann rightly points out, the New Testament confronts this good man—the man who has observed all the things of the law since his youth (Mark 10:20)—not with the option for a higher good, a higher moral standard, but rather with the demand for a qualitative change, "the reversal of the direction his will has previously had," which means to leave behind "the past as that which constantly threatens" and to become "open for the genuine future," "letting himself be determined by the future."[16]

It becomes obvious why Christians and secular men who speak the language of political humanism find themselves so often side by side. They participate in a fundamental refusal to be absorbed by systems that require adaptation to given structures. They both deny the legitimacy of all structures—either structures that claim to be based in nature, or structures that claim to represent transcendent eternal values, or structures that claim to represent the truth of technological efficacy—as the determining and final context for man's action. With their common passion for, and vision of, human deliverance, they agree that integration in systems is a form of domestication that trades security for freedom, goods for a critical consciousness, a full stomach for man's vision of a new tomorrow. The problem of humanization cannot be thus equated with economy or economic development (the great temptation of the poor nations of the world!). Humanization is not the gift either of the gods of fertility or of their resurrected form today, the goods of technology. Both agree that man does not live by bread alone. The fundamental issue at stake is whether man is free to create his own future, to break away from all the domesticating systems that strive to preserve the old and recurrent, in order to march toward a new tomorrow.

CHAPTER THREE

THE HISTORICITY OF FREEDOM

The reason why Christians and political humanists find themselves so often together in common tasks is that the languages they speak spring from a similar passion and point to a similar hope. Both languages could be described as expressive of a "passion for and vision of human deliverance."[1] What separates them is the basic historical experience in which they were formed and which determines the understanding of the context that makes possible the transformation of this vision and passion into historical reality.

The Language of Humanistic Messianism: Humanization as a Task

In the preceding analysis of the language of political humanism we indicated that it is thoroughly historical. It is born out of the experience of the pains of the world, its contradictions and negativity. It points to a historical future of humanization, in which the possibilities of human liberation that are arrested by and in the present could become historical. And finally we indicated that it is a language of freedom because it negates and hopes to the extent to which it believes that man is free and powerful enough to liberate himself from what keeps him under bondage. The language of political humanism is therefore a form of historical optimism. It takes the risk of making all its hopes for a new future for man depend on man's freedom to make history free. The passion for and vision of human liberation will become historical "by the powers of man alone."[2] Humanization is man's task. It is a form of optimism that combines a confidence in man's vocation for freedom, his determination to create a new future, and a confidence in the openness of history to this activity of man. It believes that "mankind always sets itself only such problems as it can solve; for when we look closer we will always find that the problem itself only arises when the material conditions for its solution are already present or at least in the process of coming into being."[3] Man's openness to the future is thus the indication that the future is open to him, ripe for his action. Therefore the emergence of the consciousness of "ought" coincides with the subjective and objective possibility of the "can."

The problem which the language of political humanism presents, however, is whether it is possible to remain thoroughly historical and optimistic at the same time. Can this optimism as to man, as the only creator of history, survive when confronted with the brutal fact of power in our present-day world? Are we not led to agree with Marcuse that "nothing indicates that [we may trust that the end] will be a good end [because] . . . the economic and technological capabilities of the established societies are sufficiently vast to allow for adjustments and concessions to the underdog, and their armed forces sufficiently trained and equipped to take care of emergency situations"? Marcuse indicates very well what the problem of the language of political humanism is: it does not possess any "concepts which could bridge the gap between the present and its future; holding no promise and showing no success, it remains negative."[4] We are here confronted with the terrifying possibility of a futureless world in which man's futurity is domesticated by the power of the dominating systems.

It seems to me that this is indeed a realistic assessment of our present situation. Nothing indicates that the horizons are becoming more open. On the contrary: the openness of consciousness and its emergence in history is being overcome by the repressive powers of conservatism. We live indeed amid the contradiction between the reality and impossibility of a new tomorrow. It is real as a dimension of consciousness, but it is impossible because of the exercise of power on the part of the dominating systems. "Humanistic messianism" and its passion for and vision of human deliverance by the powers of man alone is confronted thus with the alternative between, on the one hand, optimism at the expense of its thoroughly historical character, becoming thus romantic, and, on the other, faithfulness to history and the abandonment of hope, becoming then prey to cynicism generated by frustration.

The Language of Messianic Humanism: Humanization as a Gift

The language spoken by the community of faith, although dominated by the same vision of and passion for human deliverance, finds a different context for its negation, hope, and action, because it "insists that the achievement of humanization comes by the reality and power of a deliverance which occurs in history from beyond history and refuses to abandon history."[5] In other words: for messianic humanism the politics for a new tomorrow cannot be assessed by a simple statistical or quantitative evaluation of the human resources and of the power of resistance of the existing structures of domination. It holds that the politics for a new tomorrow is the business of a power which, being free from history, and therefore not being exhausted by the statistical-quantitative possibilities that history displays, is "free for" history and therefore creates possibilities which could not be dreamed of by means of calculation.

A HISTORICAL LANGUAGE

The criticism that political humanism directs against this context for negation, hope, and action of the language of messianic humanism is that it is based on a non-historical, dogmatic idea. The point of departure and reference for the task of human liberation seems to be an idea, hope, or paradigm that is not extracted from history but hovers above history and therefore cannot be verified. It would be an illusion that would dissolve the dark colors with which a realistic consciousness paints the human condition. The consequence of this posture would be that hope would be saved at the expense of efficacy. Efficacy for the transformation of history is possible only through an objective analysis of what is possible or impossible to man in a given situation. By creating an illusory context for the hope and task of liberation, messianic humanism would make efficacy impossible, thereby becoming a form of opiate. Hope would make action inefficacious or superfluous by its severance from an objective assessment of the conditions of history.

If messianic humanism is a dogmatic idea, a paradigm which is not extracted from history and which is not directed to history, it is a form of alienation. As such it has to be discarded as a form of wish fulfillment, as illusion. However, we should not be too hasty in discarding the language of messianic humanism without first examining scientifically the type of historical experience which created it and to which it points.

Language is a historical phenomenon. It is not simply a set of symbols which refer to determinate objects or actions. It expresses the self-understanding of a community in its historical context, its relationship with its world, its vocation within history. The scientific examination of the meaning of a language, therefore, is not a simple process of checking the exact relation between words on the one hand, and things and actions to which they refer, on the other. It requires rather an inquiry into the total historical experience that gave birth to the language. The language of messianic humanism is the expression of a certain historical experience. It is not a language based on a dogmatic idea extracted either from the sphere of philosophical speculation or from the experience of the revelation of the "ground of being" or "the epiphany of the eternal present." It is simply descriptive of a historical experience of human liberation.

As we indicated before, for humanistic messianism the problem of efficacy in the creation of a new tomorrow can be solved only in the context of the real possibilities immanent in history, objectively and subjectively. Liberation is possible only when there is a historical subject who decides to make himself free. And more than that: his subjective decision will become history only if he has power to overcome the objective resistance which is opposed to his project. Liberation is the creation of man alone.

The historical experience of the biblical communities, however, presented a discrepancy at this point. Their historical deliverance could not be understood from an analysis of the objective and subjective possibilities in their historical present. Why and how did a group of slaves become a people? Israel's language indicates that it was aware of the fact that its historical liberation was not the outcome of its vocation for freedom. They were not committed to a vocation to be free. On the contrary, the fleshpots of Egypt were more attractive than the faraway hope for a land of freedom. They would rather survive in bondage than die on the way toward a new tomorrow. This was the protest continuously heard during the journey through the desert. From an analysis of their consciousness one could not envisage any possibility of liberation. The objective ways seemed equally blocked. The yoke of slavery was heavy. The oppressor was militarily strong. And they, the slaves, were weak, with no weapons, with no discipline or determination. The political power of Egypt, the unsurmountable obstacles of the journey, the survival in the desert, the problem of the conquest of the land—all these elements of the situation pointed in the same direction: the future was closed.

The people of Israel, consequently, could not see their liberation either as the result of their determination to be free or as having been made possible by the circumstances. They had not made themselves free: they were forced to be free. The language of messianic humanism is nothing more than the expression of this historical experience of freedom and liberation "in spite of," when all subjective and objective possibilities of freedom immanent in history had been aborted. It is a thoroughly historical language that points to the emergence of efficacy in history in spite of man's weakness, in spite of the insurmountable strength of the powers that keep man captive. It is the language born out of the experience of historical efficacy not as the result of the power of man but as given to him, efficacy as grace, efficacy "in spite of."[6]

If the liberating event could neither be related to the people's vocation for freedom, as the effect to its cause, nor explained as an accident of historical circumstances, the people came to understand it as an act of a power from beyond history. The liberating facts were proclaimed then as God's acts. They were not simply the result of circumstance but expressions of a transcendent freedom which was wholly determined to be for a new man, a new time, a new earth. Israel, therefore, did not have an a priori idea of God and from this dogmatic idea conclude as to his action in history. On the contrary, it found itself determined to be free, in spite of itself. This was its most fundamental historical experience. From the historical reality of the liberating facts, a new language emerges as something a posteriori that speaks about God as the power of human liberation which expressed itself in and through the formative events of the life of the community.

The biblical language about God, therefore, is not descriptive of an ontology or metaphysics. It refers to what has happened, goes on, and can occur in history. Consequently, N. H. Snaith remarks, "the Hebrew does not say that Jehovah is, or that Jehovah exists, but that He does."[7] It is a language that refers to what is possible in history, from the perspective of the historical experience of the community with the power of efficacy "in spite of." Von Rad indicates that "even the earliest avowals to Jahweh were historically determined, that is, they connect the name of this God with some statement about an action in history."[8] For the Israelite, therefore, "it is . . . the objectivity of God's historical acts which are the focus of attention, not the subjectivity of inner, emotional, diffuse, and mystical experience."[9]

The language about God, thus, is a language about events, their power and their promise. This is why when the Israelite refers to God he retells the story of the events which, in the past, brought them into being as a free people. The question "Who is God?" is answered thus by telling a story:

> A wandering Aramean was my father; he went down with a few people into Egypt and there he became a nation, great, mighty, and populous. But the Egyptians treated us harshly, they afflicted us. Then we cried to Jahweh, the God of our fathers, and Jahweh heard us, and saw our affliction, our toil, and oppression. And Jahweh brought us out of Egypt with mighty hand and outstretched arm, with great terror, with signs and wonders, and brought us to this place and gave us this land, a land flowing with milk and honey (Deut 26:5-9).[10]

Theology, or the language about God, was thus the same as reciting the events that, because of their liberating power in the past, offered a ground of hope in the present. "Thus, re-telling remains the most legitimate form of theological discourse on the Old Testament,"[11] von Rad remarks.

Because the consciousness of the biblical communities emerged from and was bound to historical events, a new way of using the powers of reason was created. The Greek mind was dominated by "the urge towards a universal understanding of the world";[12] it sought to find a "uniform natural principle" of the cosmos, the *arche* in which all the contradictions of historical order are resolved in unity and rationality. It is thought which takes as its limits the truth of "what is." That which is, is rational; that which is, is truth. Thought directs its energies to the task of understanding the world. This way of thinking is totally foreign to the Hebrew mind, because it refused to leave history in the search of a meta-historical principle in which the contradictions of history are transcendentally reconciled. Theological language was, therefore, historical language[13] which was engaged "in ever-renewed reflection upon the meaning of historical events, reflection which of course always appears only in the guise of *ad hoc* interpretations."[14] If Greek thought moved dialectically from the sensible to the intelligible, from the contradictory to the rational understanding of what is, Hebrew thought saw the liberating events more as vectors which made possible an extrapolation in the direction of the future. Because the people were liberated and created in the past by the power of God, it was possible to think in the present from the perspective of the possibilities of humanization which that past experience had created. The past became the clue for the understanding of the possibilities of liberation in the context of present events. "The Israelite eye was thus trained to take human events seriously," Wright comments, "because in them was to be learned more clearly than anywhere else what God willed and what he was about."[15] Language about God or theological language was thus an attempt to read the signs of the times, to discover the liberating thrust of present-day events. Where the events were expressions of liberating efficacy "in spite of," there was their God.

The consciousness of the New Testament communities does not depart from this context. It is rather a new expression of the historical consciousness and language of the Old Testament. When Jesus started preaching "the time is fulfilled, and the Kingdom of God is at hand; repent, and believe in the Gospel" (Mark 1:14), he was not speaking a strange language. He was addressing himself to a community that was determined by history and had a historical hope. And what he announced was the immediacy of that political reality of power in which liberation was possible and offered: the Kingdom of God. The Gospel is thus the annunciation of the historical reality of the ongoing politics of God, which expressed itself not as philosophical or mystical experience but rather as a power that invades history. Jesus was confessed by the New Testament communities as one who was the "servant" (Jn 13, Ph. 2:7), who was obedient unto death (Ph. 2:8). His will was seen as subordinated to and an expression of the messianic intention of the liberating events of the Old Testament. He was the one through whom God's politics of liberation was carried out. His obedience was thus the expression of his total identification with God's messianic activity, and therefore he could be confessed as the Messiah. The Christian community understood Jesus, thus, from the "messianic criterion," as a new liberating event in the tradition of the messianic intention hinted at from the liberation and promises which the historical experience of the people presented. As the messianic events of liberation in the Old Testament were not a result of human efficacy but rather a gift, an act of power that transcended the given possibilities of history, the Christian communities saw in Jesus an act of God's freedom. We do not find in the consciousness of the Christian community any place for messianism as evolving from the human reality.[16] Man does not produce the "logos" and "power" of human liberation out of the previously given reality. On the contrary, the power that creates a new future is something new, it is freedom from beyond history, which becomes history; it is freedom from history that is freedom for history. Only thus do the messianic power and hope for history remain as such. "The 'Logos' became flesh" (Jn 1:14). "The revealing power of the predicate flesh," Barth comments, "stands or falls with the free action of the subject Logos."[17] To paraphrase: the possibility of human liberation in history stands or falls with the free action in history of the messianic power from beyond history.

The language of the New Testament community, consequently, remains as the recital of liberating historical events. It proclaimed historical events, events that made man free, that made possible a new self-understanding so radical as to be called a "new birth" (cf. Jn 3:3), events which indicated that God was actively engaged in a struggle against the powers that kept man captive. The Gospel was thus an "act," a new insertion of freedom into history which opens new horizons for human liberation. This is why the proclamation of the Gospel announces salvation, a new possibility of human life. The language of theology remains derived from history and committed to history.

A LANGUAGE OF FREEDOM

The fact that the biblical communities were created and determined by liberating historical events led them to have a unique understanding of history, as the history of freedom. As we indicated before, the experience of historical events as formative and liberating did not allow the community of faith simply to see them as the result of accident or circumstance. They were acts, that is, events determined by freedom and therefore events which bore freedom in themselves. They presented, consequently, new exits from the enclosed circle of "what was," new openings towards different historical possibilities. Time, therefore, ceased to be considered simply as the continuum of the system of natural causality and became the creation of the will. God's will created time, it created the "ultimate ground of man's life." "But will by its nature is future-regarding, future-seeking, future-creating."[18] The time created by this future-determined will is thus the time of a project. But project means to emerge from identity with "what is." It means both will's freedom from the power of the world of the present and will's freedom for a new future to be created. To be involved in God's time is thus to participate in a present that determines itself for the creation of a new tomorrow. The will of God could never, therefore, be invoked in order to justify the status quo.

"It is the will of God," says the religious man, adjusting himself to his captivity. The will of God is here the justification of what is. It explains the necessity of what is by referring it to the divine causality and to the divine reconciliation of the historical contradictions. When the language of messianic humanism refers to the will of God, however, it is rather indicating that because time expresses the pressure of the spirit, of freedom, as it seeks its goal, it can never be stopped. Therefore, every present must be experienced as time-toward-the-new-tomorrow.[19] The new tomorrow is thus the sole determination of the present.

God is thus experienced as the presence of the future. He is freedom, in history, which makes it transcend its present form toward a new possibility of human liberation. God is not, therefore, as Moltmann aptly points out, the presence of eternity which dissolves history, the "epiphany of the eternal present." He is future-determined. As against Moltmann, however, the biblical communities did not know a God whose essential nature was the future, the *primum movens* ahead of history. The Old and the New Testaments speak about the historical present of God. The pure futuricity of God is a new form of Docetism in which God loses the present dimension and therefore becomes ahistorical. The messianic possibilities of history for both the Old and the New Testaments depend on the fact that God has a present. For the Old Testament one can hope because "the Lord your God is in the midst of you" (Deut 8:21); for the New, hope is derived from the historicity, the incarnation of God. A God who is always future is a God who does not become historical in terms of power but who remains ahead, attracting history to himself by means of eros. The biblical communities, however, had a hope for the future because God was present, and in his present, through the exercise of power, which was historical through and through, he negated historically and presently the power of "what was," thereby making man and history open for a new tomorrow. God was thus experienced as present determined toward the future, and God's acts, consequently, created a present in which the future was being formed.

This was proclaimed by Jesus in many of his parables, that "the future is now at work secretly, as a germinating seed, or spreading leaven, or ripening harvest. As such it is actually present as the external, tangible phenomena which men see and hear."[20] Albert Schweitzer indicated that this was the dominating motif of Jesus' life. He not only announced the imminent breaking in of the future as something which was God's business alone. His ministry was more than that: it was action intended to force the future to become present.[21] He could not therefore behave in terms of the present, taking the sphere of "what was" as the context for his words and deeds. He behaved as in an interim, on the way between the today and the tomorrow, and therefore his ethic was both expressive of the presence of the future and was to function as the midwife of the future. Schweitzer gives to this interpretation a totally negative evaluation because he believed that this type of behavior was ahistorical and only possible if one lives "wholly in dogmatic history"[22] which makes man indifferent to and alienated from the real possibilities which the actual historical context presents.[23] However, it is possible to understand the life of Jesus differently, as the expression of obedience to the God who is the presence of the future, who pushes the present towards new possibilities of judgment and human liberation. As we tried to indicate, this is not a dogmatic idea but rather an inference from the historical experience of the people.

When Jesus said that the Kingdom of God was at hand and behaved in such a way as to force the irruption of the future, he was simply thinking and behaving in the tradition of the messianic humanism of the Old Testament. There is an evident emphasis on the present. *Now* is the time of obedience. *Now* "the blind receive their sight, the lame walk, lepers are cleansed, the deaf hear, the dead are raised up, the poor have good news preached to them" (Luke 7:22). But that present had something special. It was not the presence of the eternal now, a present that exhausted itself. The future did not become present in an eternal now as in realized eschatology. Nor did it remain an isolated dogmatic idea, independent from and not related to the now, as a future that comes down from the heavens, as with consistent eschatology. The now was the time when a liberating activity that pushed toward the future was going on. Already and not yet were not, therefore, abstract points in the chronology of objective time. The not yet was what qualified and determined the present. It was not primarily the point of arrival but rather that which was being engendered in the womb of the present. In the now we have the presence of the future made historical through God's action. God is thus neither the "eternal present" or the "absolute future" for the community of faith. It came to see, from its historical experience, that what God's action does is to create an explosiveness that is both present and negates the present. Because God acts, "every situation is pregnant with ultimate possibility; every moment is made explosive by the presence of an infinite power."[24] "We know," says Paul (Rom 8:22), that the whole creation is groaning in travail until now. And not only the creation, but we ourselves, who have the first fruits of the Spirit, groan inwardly as we wait for adoption as sons, the redemption of our bodies. For in this hope we are saved." Man and creation are united together in a "symphony of groaning," having the "Spirit as the conductor" (Hoekendijk). The Spirit has given us the "first fruits," the "aperitif" (Hoekendijk) which makes creation and man, together, long for redemption. Man and creation are thus pregnant, having within themselves a new life, a new tomorrow, engendered by the Spirit which, in the words of Paul, "dwells in you" (8:11). It is because the Spirit is present that the reality of the presence of the future, the groaning of travail and the reality of hope are created. We hope, we are determined for the future, because we are pregnant. We are "infected" with the presence of the future.[25]

The historical time created by God's messianic activity is thus radically opposed to organic time, the time of nature. In organic time the present receives the past, nay the present emerges from the past by repetition or evolution. The present is thus the presence of the past. Within historical time, however, the past that was about to determine the present is penetrated by freedom. Through this act the unfolding of the immanent possibilities of "what was" is interrupted and the new is inserted into the present. The present becomes thus a pregnancy in which a new future already determines the present toward a historical tomorrow. The future is therefore being engendered now, amid the history where man is living, compelling him to respond to the vectors of the events that are bearers of freedom. Hope is possible and real because now, in the center of history, new historical liberating events are being created. Paraphrasing A. V. Pinto, we may say that this hope does not come from the perception of a pattern prior to the perception of the facts, and for this reason eternal. . . . This hope is induced from the opening events in history. It is therefore empirical, derived from history and only thus can it act as the midwife of the future that now exists only as pregnancy. This paraphrase took as its model the language of political humanism and its determination for hope. It is remarkable how it runs parallel to the biblical understanding of hope as being induced from historical events. Biblical hope, its origin and nature cannot be understood, therefore, "if we start from 'eschatology,' that is to say from a doctrine or conception of the 'last things,' " observes Buber. Hope not derived from and related to what is going on here and now has nothing to do with the biblical historical ways of thinking; it is speculation, "dogmatic idea," which misses the "special, concrete, historical core [of biblical hope, since this hope] does not belong to the margin of history where it vanishes into the realms of the timeless, but it belongs to the center, ever-changing center, that is to say, it belongs to the experienced hour and its possibility."[26]

At this point it is necessary to indicate the problematic character of the interpretations of the future in Barth and Moltmann. For Barth the future is formally and actually already ahead of us. The historical events in the present, therefore, do not mediate a new future. The future is not born out of the present. On the contrary, the now and man's freedom acquire their significance when they are an imitation of, and play under the light of, the future that is revealed to man. Moltmann attempted to correct this, but he still affirms that the future, although not ontologically, is formally ready and as such moves the present by attraction towards itself. For both of them, however, the present does not mediate the future.

Our exploration, however, has led us to reach a different conclusion: that the future is mediated into history through the present, that the present is where the future is being formed. History is thus the medium in and through which God creates for history, man, and himself, a future that does not yet exist, either actually or formally. The language of messianic humanism about God is therefore a language about an ongoing activity in which the present is broken open—really open—toward the new. But the other side must be underlined as well: it is only in the context of the ongoing politics of God that it is possible to speak about the future and hope. The subjective possibility of hope is thus a counter-part and response to the activity that makes history objectively open for a new tomorrow.

THE LANGUAGE OF HUMANISM

The God to whom the language of messianic humanism refers is thus a humanist. The language speaks of "the humanity of God."[27] His name is a symbol for "what it takes to make and to keep human life human in the world." The community of faith, therefore, cannot answer the question about God except by telling what he has done for man. The shape of its God is thus a human shape because his action in history is the action that makes room for, indeed forces, man to become human. It is not, therefore, the language of metaphysics, the language about a realm beyond history. It remains historical. It describes when and how man was made free. And remaining strictly historical, it extrapolates the past experience of human liberation into the present and future and finds in this historical context the answer to the question: "What is necessary to make and to keep human life human in the world?"

What separates humanistic messianism from messianic humanism is not, therefore, that one is historical and the other is not. Both are historical. The difference between them is that humanistic messianism is born out of a historical experience in which only the statistically and quantitatively tangible resources of man's freedom and determination are available, whereas messianic humanism was created by the historical reality of liberation in spite of the collapse of all human resources. Humanistic messianism thus starts with man. Because man is the only resource it has at its disposal, he is the object of its trust and hope. It stands or falls with the transcending powers of man. These are the powers, the only powers, available for human liberation. Messianic humanism, on the contrary, believes, from its historical experience, in the humanizing determination of the transcendent. When it pronounces the name "God," it is referring to the power for humanization that remains determined to make man historically free even when all objective and subjective possibilities immanent in history have been exhausted. Feuerbach's statements that "the beginning, middle, and the end of religion is man" and that "the true sense of Theology is Anthropology"—statements expressive of the optimism and hope of humanistic messianism as to man as his own liberator—find in messianic humanism a new form. The beginning, middle, and end of God's activity is the liberation of man. To speak about God is to speak about the historical events that made and make man free.

The community of faith referred to this fact by using the word "grace." It means that the only God about whom the language of faith speaks is the One who is totally determined for man. This is why Luther stubbornly refused to allow the language of theology to be concerned about a God who had not given himself historically to man. To speak correctly about God is to speak about One who does not have any other mode of determination save that of being for man. For Luther, consequently, the language of theology was simply the description of a historical person who exhausts the self-determination of God: Jesus Christ. "He is the election," the self-determination "of God before which and beside which God cannot make any other choices," Barth comments. He "must still be understood as truly the beginning of all God's ways and works."[28] In the language of the community of faith about God we have thus the convergence of history, messianism, and humanism. The language is historical. It describes the events that historically are bearers of human liberation. They are bearers of human liberation, however, not by the powers of man alone, but by the power of God who determines himself to be only for man, by the grace of the Messiah. And, determined by God's freedom for man and for history, man finds the possibility of living as a free man, in and for history. Messianism is thus the presupposition for humanism. Going back to Luther: it is only in the context of the God who is totally free for man that we can speak about the freedom of the Christian man for life. We must never forget, however, that the language of the community of faith about Jesus emerges from the historical experience of the messianic activity which makes man free. It is in this context that Jesus is to be understood, as the power and as the norm of God's historical politics of human liberation. So that, when we speak about Jesus we are speaking about history, about the ongoing politics of grace in history and consequently about the triumph of the human in history.

We pointed out that humanistic messianism stands or falls with its belief in the transcending powers of man as the only powers available for human liberation. We remarked, moreover, that the dilemma of humanistic messianism today, because of the domestication of consciousness and the power of the structures that hold the present captive, is either history without hope, realism and the cynicism of despair, on the one hand, or hope without history, romanticism at the expense of the realistic assessment of present day historical situation, on the other. Messianic humanism rejects both alternatives: never hope without history; never history without hope. It remains realistic without despair and hopeful without being romantic. It makes possible for man to remain as man, in history, without losing hope, hoping against hope, in the expectation that the messianic politics of God will bring to man and history a new future and a new hope.

CHAPTER FOUR

THE DIALECTICS OF FREEDOM

Humanistic messianism and messianic humanism are both dominated by the love and vision of human deliverance. Human deliverance, however, is not yet historical, it cannot be found as a reality
in the present. It exists now as a project of the will. Therefore, it
can be expressed only in the language of hope, in the universe of
discourse which speaks not about the actual in history but about that
which is possible to history. For both of them, therefore, the alternative, hope without history and history without hope, are equally
abominable, since they mean that human liberation is impossible in
history. The project of human liberation and with it both humanistic messianism and messianic humanism would thus be proved to
be nonsense, since the language of human liberation is meaningful
only if it refers to a project born out of history and which is possible
in history. In other words: hope has to be the language of the
possible, if it is to inform and determine ethics as the science and
activity that aims at the historization of hope. Hope therefore cannot be confused with fantasy or illusion, because it is derived from
history and envisions, from the experience of the past, what is
possible to history. It is the extrapolation into the future of man's
historical experience with the politics of freedom in the past. In
hope reason does not play the function of describing "what is." It
is no longer "conformed to this world" but rather free for the
criticism of "what is" for the sake of that which could be. Consequently, "hope alone is to be called 'realistic,'" observes Moltmann, "because it alone takes seriously the possibilities with which

all reality is fraught. It does not take things as they happen to stand or to lie, but as progressing, moving things with possibilities of change. . . . [Hope is thus] a realistic way of perceiving the scope of our real possibilities."[1] Reason dominated by hope sees the real through the experience with the liberating activity of freedom in the world, as a politics which "gives life to the dead and calls into existence the things that do not exist" (Rom 4:17). The real is that which, through freedom, can be. For reason without hope the real is the brute reality of "what is" as the ultimate datum of its experience. It does not make room, therefore, for the activity that aims at overcoming the inhuman of "what is" in order to create a new and more human reality. Hope, consequently, expresses what is possible to history and therefore what can be made historical through the activity of freedom, only to the extent to which it is derived from and is an extrapolation of the objective movement of the politics of human liberation, as experienced in history. In other words: it is not enough to say that freedom opens its way towards the future in history; hope emerges when we are able to see how freedom moves on its way. Only thus does it serve ethics. Only thus is it a realistic way of perceiving history.

For the sake of hope and human liberation it is therefore of the utmost importance to unmask the pseudo-hopes, visions of the future that are not derived from the reading of the objective movement of the politics of freedom in history. Visions of the future not extracted from history or which do not take the movement of freedom as their basis, cannot be called hope: they are forms of alienation, illusions which cannot inform history because of their unrelatedness to the way of operation of freedom in the world.

This is one of the reasons why humanistic messianism maintains a polemic with religion: it offers to man a hope not derived from history, a hope that hovers above and beyond history, and which is not mediated through the activity of freedom in history. Because it is not extracted from history it does not point to what is historically possible. Instead of making man free for history, it rather uproots him from it. Hope would be here a compensation for the impotence of freedom and the expression of man's despair of the possibilities of history. It would be a creation of the inability of man's subjectivity to come to terms with its own frustrations, but not the result of its experience with the objective liberating movement of freedom.

Humanistic messianism and messianic humanism have as well a polemic with the idea of progress and the hope it implies. This is rather strange, because it seems that there is no hope that could claim to be as based on historical facts and more faithful to what is possible to history than that presented by the idea of progress. The modern idea of progress is the result of an extrapolation of the experience of the emergence of reason in history, as the man of the Enlightenment understood it. Mankind had reached a stage in which reason finally disentangled itself from the irrational and instinctive. Free from the irrational, reason was believed to be the lord of history. There was the future of man, like a block of marble, waiting to be given a shape according to the verdict of reason as to what was right. From the historical experience of the liberation of reason, man then turned his eyes to the future and was able to envisage the new world he was now free to create. It is true that this naive optimism has been to a great extent destroyed by the historical experiences of our century. But not completely, because now, as never before, the same spirit of optimism as to progress has become embodied in technological reason, as the messianism of technology, as technologism. From the point of view of the messianism of technology the world lies wide open ahead of man, simply waiting for the "technique" that will make his hopes historical reality. It cannot say that it does not possess any "concepts which could bridge the gap between the present and the future." It knows how to do it. It believes, therefore, that ideology is no longer necessary as a tool for the creation of the future. Bondage is overcome by wisdom and knowledge.

The problem with the messianism of technology and the idea of progress, from the perspective of the historical experience of humanistic messianism and messianic humanism, is that the rationality operative in technology is not derived from the experience with the liberating movement of freedom in history but rather from the rationality of nature. It makes room for the quantitatively different but not for the qualitatively new. It is a rationality that depends on quantitative changes to survive but dies if qualitative changes occur. Progress or economic development, as the creation of technology, would thus become a different sort of opiate that would prevent qualitative changes, changes created by freedom, by making freedom tamed through the marvels and power of the quantitative factor. It would make freedom domesticated, thereby destroying it as freedom. It would make the sphere of what is possible to history shrink to what is allowed by the technological system. Because this vision of hope is not extracted from the history of freedom but rather from the paradigm of nature, history, as the history of freedom, comes to an end.

The hope of human liberation, the hope for the qualitatively new, the hope which is to be the child of freedom, can be thought of only when one discovers how freedom in the past has mediated the new and liberating to history.

Messianic humanism and humanistic messianism cannot therefore accept any type of hope save the hope that is concretely derived from their vision of the how of freedom in history, of the way whereby it is able to overcome the old and enslaving and thereby make room for the new and liberating. And the historical experience of both of them indicates one thing: freedom creates the new in history through a dialectical process. The new is not mediated directly. The reason for this is that the old, in history, resists and opposes the new. As a consequence, the Yes that freedom addresses to the new becomes historical only through and beyond the No with which it confronts, resists, and overcomes the power of the old that wants to perpetuate itself and abort the new. Nietzsche captured the movement of the dialectic of liberation in a parable of the three metamorphoses of the spirit.[2] In the first phase the spirit appears as a camel, the beast of burden that wants to be well loaded. It does not know how to say "No." It is submerged into, reconciled with, and domesticated by what is. It takes the given upon itself and carries it. It is the oppressed, unfree consciousness that is at one with the world in which it emerged. The only word it is able to say is "Yes." But then freedom emerges. The spirit becomes a lion. The lion is the power of freedom that has learned to say "No" to the master who kept it under bondage. Who is this master? It is the great dragon "Thou shalt," which lies in the way of freedom, sparkling like gold, an animal covered with the scales "thou shalt." "All value of all things shines on me," it says. "All value has long been created, and I am all created value." Why is the lion necessary? For the creation of freedom, which cannot exist without the resistance of the No to the power that holds the past as the ultimate reality. The old must be broken, the dragon must be killed, otherwise the new cannot live. When it confronts the power of the old, freedom assumes then the form of negation. But the lion is not the final expression of freedom. The spirit becomes a child. "Why must the preying lion still become a child?" asks Nietzsche. "The child is innocence and forgetting, a new begin-ning, a game, a self-propelled wheel, a first movement, a sacred 'Yes.' . . . For the game of creation . . . a sacred 'Yes' is needed."[3] Once the old is deprived of its power to enslave and paralyze, the world is made open for experimentation, for the creation of the new tomorrow. Freedom, accordingly, is not a movement emerg-ing from or within the boundaries of the given system. It is rather the insertion of a new reality into history in such a way that the closed present is broken open for the new.

The possibility of liberation and the shape of hope is thus derived from the perception of the conflicting character of the process whereby freedom opens its way toward the new. The movement can be summarized in three moments:

First: the reality of the old as power used for self-preservation, against the new, as violence.

Second: freedom as power against the violence of preservation, as the negation of the negative.

Third: freedom as power for creation of the new, for ex-perimentation, as affirmation.

Humanistic messianism and messianic humanism thus agree not only in their common passion for and vision of human libera-tion but also as to the dynamics whereby freedom mediates this hope into history. Again what separates them is the basic historical experience that formed them. They hope, therefore, from a differ-ent assessment of what it is that is possible to freedom, and there-fore of what it is that is possible to history.

Humanistic messianism sees the dialectic of freedom as intrinsically and exclusively determined by the dialectic of the material relations in society. Consequently, only to the extent that man suffers the contradictions of the material relations and consciously becomes aware of this contradiction does he emerge as the power that negates in order to overcome. In this context, he has a free consciousness committed to the project of transforming its hope of liberation in historical reality. He is the revolutionary. Human liberation is thus the creation of the powers of man alone, and the historization of hope depends exclusively on the determination of his will. However, present-day technological society confronts man with two new elements: first, its ability to overcome the material contradictions of society, if not actually at least virtually. It displays, therefore, the power of eliminating opposition, of eliminating the pain of the contradictions. The goods it distributes function as the opiate of the people. It thus makes consciousness unable to say "No." And second, it has concentrated in the hands of the masters such a massive amount of power that it seems that they are now able to destroy the negative powers of society. The dragon devours the lion. The hope of humanistic messianism, consequently, faces the danger of collapse. Humanistic messianism is then confronted with the options that are the negation of itself: hope without history or history without hope. By the powers of man alone man hopes without confidence: "nothing indicates that the end will be a good end." There is no promise that freedom will succeed in its painful dialectical movement towards man's liberation. It is in this context that the historical experience of messianic humanism with the dialectics of freedom offers a different assessment of what is possible to history, thereby providing a different ground for the hope of human liberation.

The Negative in History: The Politics That Aborts the New Tomorrow

The language of human liberation has its roots in the present. It speaks from the pains of a present which wants to become free but which is not allowed to transform its project into history. Its universe of discourse is therefore determined, on the one hand, by the freedom of the consciousness that existentially feels the inhuman contradictions of the present and hopes for a new tomorrow in which they will be overcome, and on the other hand, by the reality of frustration and despair created by the objective conditions of power in history, which abort the attempts of human liberation. It is this historical reality that requires theological investigation, born out of history, which remains faithful to and inserted into history and which is made for the sake of human liberation. The task is simply to examine this historical phenomenon, namely, the exercise of political power that makes impossible human liberation, from the perspective of the historical experience of the community of faith and for the sake of the creation of a new tomorrow for the man who today is kept captive.

We indicated earlier that the theological language of the community of faith was the creation of its experience with liberating events which, together, could be described as the history of freedom. Their history, however, presented another datum, side by side with the history of freedom: the history of unfreedom.[4] Man proved historically to be unable to live as if surfing on the waves of the political dynamics that pushes toward the future. Consequently, what man did was not expressive of his freedom for the future but rather of his fear of the future. His actions were an attempt to escape from freedom, from the open horizons that lead to an uncertain future. The language that describes what man does points therefore to his rebellion, to his refusal to act in response to the liberating dynamics of the politics of God. It points to his fall from history to nature. The people who had been made free, who had experienced the exhilarating possibilities of a future-determined life, traded freedom for security, the openness of historical horizons for the warmth of the womb of nature. A strange metamorphosis then occurred: the "bride" became a "harlot," the "vine of pure seed" turned out to be degenerate and wild, the son who was the object of God's love bowed down to the gods of nature, becoming like a wild ass, like a young camel in her lust. Right on the journey toward the future the true voice of man is heard: rather the fleshpots of Egypt than the danger of the journey towards the promised land (Ex 16:3).[5] This process of degeneration from history to nature was so overwhelming that it was generalized into the myth of the fall.[6] Set in the provisional and finite context of human life, man fears the future. He fears life. He is unable to proceed with faith, acting in abandonment and trust. The future is the possibility of death. In the context of trust in God man would be able to act in freedom and therefore to be free for life. But since he cannot trust, the reality of insecurity and death become the *factors*, the powers that create the fact of his behavior. He cannot hope, because hope is to be freedom for the future. But the future he sees is not friendly and inviting but rather threatening. He has to "unlearn hope" (Hoekendijk). His activity, therefore, becomes a frenetic striving "to forestall the future . . . and to keep what now is for the future."[7] Because man could not trust, in the context of love, the liberation and humanization of God's politics, now he finds himself with the titanic task of avoiding the future over which he has no control, by absolutizing his past and his present, by making what he does the ultimate ground for his own humanization.[8] Since he is unable to be free for the future because of his lack of confidence, he wants to liberate himself from history. He wants to be like God, that is, to be the creator of his own history, the sole center that determines the conditions of humanization. His lack of faith issues then in the pride of self-affirmation. He becomes his own messiah. His subjectivity dominated by his fear of the future projects itself then toward the world of time and space. It becomes history. It creates history. But the history thereby created bears the stamp of the unfreedom toward the future that generated it. It is history that is the child of the power of pride, created in the image and likeness of the man who is afraid of freedom and consequently cannot hope.

As Augustine pointed out, we have a new political reality, the "city of man," which is the objective counterpart of man's decision of not determining himself for history, for others, but rather according to his *amor sui*, for himself. History is the field of his self-affirmation. The objective structures he creates in the world, then, are projections of his own fear and unfreedom and therefore intended to be defenses against freedom and the future. Instead of being the starting point for experimentation, they come to be the end of experimentation. The tendency of human institutions, therefore, is to leave behind the openness from which they started, and to become closed, frozen, finished, "ontocratic" (van Leeuwen).[9] It seems to me that this process of fall from history to nature is very instructive for our understanding of what happened with technology. At first technology was a tool, an instrument in man's hand for the building of a different and new world. It was, therefore, a revolutionary instrument that could be rightly said to be the bearer of the future. The instrument, however, became a system, the technological society. And this transition from instrument in the hands of man's freedom to the system which now provides the rules that freedom has to obey, is what explains why what yesterday was an instrument for liberation has today become the creator of the one-dimensional man and of all sorts of international exploitation, oppression, and repression.

Augustine called these systems built by *amor sui* and the love of power "private forms *of good.*" They entice man to the extent to which they are able to offer him something good. The "children of darkness" display a remarkable ability to produce "great" or "utopian societies." Who could dream of anything, any system that could promise and offer more than the technological system does? Examined from the point of view of its quantitative performance, the private forms of good seem to be unsurpassable in their production of goods. Nature seems to triumph over history. In order to come to understand what is the true meaning of these private forms of good one cannot, however, allow oneself to be put under the spell of the production and distribution of its goods. One has to pay attention to the fact that they are *private* forms of good. Their own good is their sole concern. The first question that determines all the decisions is the question of national or class self-interest. The interests of the group or nation become the ultimate criterion for the judgment of everything that is to happen in the world. Reinhold Niebuhr, in his *Moral Man and Immoral Society*[10] pointed out that groups and nations do not act from love and justice but fundamentally in terms of egoism. Justice becomes what serves the economic, military, and political interests of the nation.

What is just and true economically? It is what makes the master more affluent and the nations he exploits more dependent on and dominated by him. What is just and true politically? It is the use of power that will destroy everything "dangerous to the peace and safety" of the master, everything that is "a manifestation of an unfriendly disposition towards him," everything that is "endangering his peace and happiness."[11] The "principle of self-preservation," self-aggrandizement, and expansion are thus the laws of the master, no matter how he attempts to justify himself. "The moral attitudes of dominant and privileged groups," R. Niebuhr notes, "are characterized by universal self-deception and hypocrisy. . . . The intelligence of privileged groups is usually applied to the task of inventing specious proofs for the theory that universal values spring from, and that general interests are served by, the special privileges which they hold."[12] It was Augustine who first saw that what the dominant political groups call right or legality is not justice but rather the transformation of their will to power and the selfish and plundering rule of their behavior into the law that is forcibly imposed upon those whom they dominate. Law, consequently, is not the expression of the divine world of eternal values as Greeks and Romans believed but rather the historical creation of the politics of the city of man, dominated by *amor sui*, pride, and will to power.[13]

By raising its will to power to the status of law, the nation or class absolutizes itself. "Thou art my God." This becomes then the confession of faith which the man who is afraid of freedom addresses to the political and legal structures his unfreedom has created. Through this claim "human pride and self-assertion reach their ultimate form and seek to break all bounds of finiteness."[14] And the class and nation come to behave as though they were the embodiment of truth and justice and that, therefore, they are destined to eternity. Their first priority is, consequently, self-preservation, through the destruction of the powers that threaten their project of self-perpetuation. As Niebuhr remarks, their first concern is with the preservation of their power—stability—and not with justice. The fear of freedom that created structures which were to defend the self against the threat of the future now assumes a different form: it uses the structures it created in order to affirm itself as the master of those not included within the limits of the private form of good of which it is the center. The world of free man gives place to a world of masters and slaves. The master, as Berdjaev properly remarks, is not free. He is afraid of the future and this is the reason why he wants to dominate. Because he is afraid, he does not want to see his fellow man be free. The freedom of the other man is a threat to his own will to power. The "order of life in which all created things are instrumental to the possibility and the power given to man—through fellowship with God—to be himself in being related to his fellow man, has been inverted by the will to power by which man subdues his environment, including his 'brother,'" Lehmann remarks.[15] Man's power is no longer an expression of freedom but a projection of his concern to keep himself for the future even if this requires that the neighbor be denied the right to his own future. Power is here an expression not of love and justice but of the pride that springs from the unfree man. The "arrogance of power" (to use Senator William Fulbright's term) then transforms the neighbor, be he a man or a nation, into a means to the ends that *amor sui* sets for itself, as the sole center of the world.

The fear of the future then gives birth to violence. What is violence? It is easy to understand that two completely different answers can be given to this question. From the point of view of the man who is afraid of the future and who, therefore, has built structures to defend himself against it, violence is everything that disturbs or threatens the world his fear has built. Everything that tends to usher in the new, that moves toward change, everything that opposes the structures that claim to be destined for eternity, is violence. The power such a man exercises against the man or nation whom he dominates is not violence because it is exercised in order to preserve himself. And since his sole concern is his self-preservation, the pains and sufferings of the others do not enter into his calculation as to his use of power.

From the viewpoint of the man who is free for the future, violence is a totally different reality. It is whatever denies him a future, whatever aborts his project to create a new tomorrow; it is the power that keeps him prisoner of the futureless structures of a futureless world. Violence is the power of defuturization, which strives to close man's consciousness to the future and the future to man's consciousness. Violence is the power that denies to man the possibility of exercising his freedom for himself, by making it a function of the project of the master. He wants to build a new future, but since his master dominates him, everything he does, instead of bringing about the future he hopes for, makes the presence of his master more tyrannical. He is thus dehistorized, since he is made impotent to create his history. He becomes an object, and does not create but rather reacts to the stimuli that come to him from his master.

The situation of the nations of the Third World which are under the colonial or neo-colonial domination of the Western affluent powers is a painful illustration of what violence does. We often think that the violence of colonialism is exploitation and that its result is poverty and underdevelopment. This is true, but it is not the whole truth. The most basic form of the violence of colonialism is that it defuturized and defuturizes the nations under its power. These nations were and are being denied the freedom to plan their own future. They were forced to be sub-systems of the colonial "private forms of good," thereby becoming the world proletariat. The lives of their people, instead of being planned according to the human exigencies of their situation, were forced to react reflexively to the demands of the economy of the masters. The future was the monopoly of the master and no future that would endanger the master's project was allowed them. They were robbed of nature and of the future.

Today the masters are willing to make concessions. They will allow the black man to be "integrated" and to participate in the goods of the masters' world. They will allow the poor nations to participate in some of the fruits—the surplus—of the economy of the great societies. They are willing to offer plans and aid for economic development. All these concessions, however, are made with a definite condition: that the slaves will remain slaves, that they will not liberate themselves, that they will not be allowed to say no to the masters. The masters are able to improve the conditions of the slave, to give him more of "nature," but they refuse to give him freedom. The international economic relations of trade between rich and poor countries indicate that the latter are becoming more and more dependent, more and more dominated by the violence of defuturization. Egypt promises more abundant flesh pots to the slaves, provided that the slaves forget about their project of liberation.

The violence of the private forms of good, for the sake of their self-perpetuation, accordingly triumphs when it succeeds in making the future closed to consciousness and the consciousness closed to the future. And as it celebrates its triumph, a strange thing occurs: it becomes almost impossible to find violence, because its total triumph takes the form of a total peace. The men and nations afraid of the future desire nothing more earnestly than peace, peace on their own terms, the peace of the slave who gives up hope. There is peace in hopelessness; when man loses hope he is no longer alive, he cannot project. His reason does not have the conditions under which to think about a new tomorrow, nor does his will have the determination to try what hope has abandoned. History comes to an end. The master remains master; the slave remains slave. There is peace.

This is the politics of fear of the future, the politics of the preservation of the yesterday and of the abortion of the future. But we have indicated above that God's presence in the world is the presence of the future. The presence of the past and the presence of the future cannot coexist. The incarnation, therefore, has the character of confrontation. "The encounter of divine grace and human sin has the nature of a collision,"[16] G. Hendry observes. From this perspective the cross assumes an imminently political character. It does not stand simply for the tragedy of death or finitude, which are phenomena of nature. The fact is that Christ did not simply die. "Man put him to death. They rejected him and killed him because they hated him."[17] Finitude and death, categories of nature, are here set in the historical context of the politics that defuturizes man. Christ was killed as a subversive, condemned as a criminal, as a threat to the order of society, by the powers that represented the highest in law and political order, on the one hand,

and law and piety, on the other. He is crucified by *Roma aeterna*,[18] which had established its *pax* over the whole *oikoumene*. And his condemnation was demanded by and received the approval of religion. Law and order face freedom as a threatening presence, as subversion of their sacred and final character. Law and order want to close; freedom wants to open. Law and order want to preserve the old; freedom wants to create the new. The presence of the future is therefore the object of hatred because it relativizes, desacralizes, judges, and ultimately abrogates the ultimacy and messianic pretensions of the powers that dominate the established order. When law and piety kill the presence of the future they thereby reveal what they are: the violence of the old that destroys the new and brings history to its end. They embody the dynamics of the politics of the Anti-Christ, the one who wants to kill the Messiah, the presence of the future.

History thus is not an open process in which the consciousness that is free for the future finds a future that is free for it. On the contrary, the way is blocked by a politics of violence that makes the historization of human liberation impossible.

The Negation of the Negative: The Suffering God

The vision of the violent and repressive character of the politics that wants to forestall the future in order to preserve a world of master and slaves leads us to a conclusion that seems contradictory and even absurd: the slaves, the wretched of the earth, the outcasts and marginals, those who are not in but rather under the private forms of good created by man's will to power, these are those who can have the vision and passion for and are able to understand the language of hope, freedom, and liberation. The slave is the one who suffers in his own flesh the defuturization which the master's structures of domination impose upon him. He is the one who lives in the knowledge of what death is because in his life he experiences the death of hopelessness and futurelessness which, from the master's will to preservation, are preconditions for his fight against the threatening future he wants to forestall. Because his present is the suffering of futurelessness, the slave is made free for the risk of a new future that promises life. Against the master's will to power he draws from his bondage his will to freedom. It is thus amid the suffering and impotence of the slave whose future is taken away by his master that the negation of the present and the hope for the new are born. Perhaps this is why the Gospel is so skeptical about the wealthy and powerful, to the point of exclaiming: How difficult is it for a rich man to enter the kingdom of God! The rich and powerful want to preserve their "now." The kingdom, on the contrary, is the presence of the future that forces men out of every "now" toward a new tomorrow. The suffering of the slave, however, is no virtue. If it were, the slave would have to find his happiness in the act of his suffering. He could not have the right to hope to overcome it. Suffering is rather the starting point for the dialectics of liberation that negates the old and stretches itself, in hope, toward the new. It is the negation of the negative. It is because the structures of defuturization make man suffer by making him a being without hope, that their negative, anti-human character is revealed. And it is because man suffers that the negative is negated, rejected, right in the act of suffering.

Humanistic messianism proceeds in the confidence that the consciousness that suffers will remain negative, protesting, as the contradictory and subversive presence. It draws its hope from its confidence that the slave will never become domesticated by his slavery. If the slave comes to ignore the death of his present and is able to find enjoyment and happiness in it, he ceases to be the liberating power of history. With the happy slave the history of liberation comes to an end, since his will to freedom is no longer opposed to the master's will to power. The threatening aspect of the technological society is found exactly here, in its ability to unify the opposites, making the slave grateful to the master for the goods he is allowed to enjoy in his captivity. The master ceases to be the power to be resisted, and becomes the "giver" of the slave's life. He becomes the god of the slave. The Negro is allowed—yes, allowed; this is his master's concession!—to enjoy the fruits of the white society which had made him suffer. The nations that have been under the power of the affluent lands are promised a share in the fruits of the private forms of good which the latter's will to power has built. Their slavery becomes therefore the source of their liberation because they are then absolved from the task of building their own future as they accept the present the masters promise. Plunged into the goods of affluence, the slave finds a happiness that makes him oblivious of the wretchedness of his futurelessness.

This is why messianic humanism refuses to draw its hope from the slave's faithfulness to the protest that is intrinsic to his condition of slave. Its historical experience shows that those who once were the negative slaves, and therefore the bearers of freedom, become, once they achieve their freedom, dominated by concern for the preservation of their present and are then infected with the sin of their masters: they are now those who want to forestall the future. It is this phenomenon that led André Gide to comment that "there is no greater conservative than a revolutionary in power." But more than that: messianic humanism knows from its historical experience that the slave very often finds his happiness in his bondage. It knows about the power of the oppressive structures of domination to create an oppressed consciousness that unlearns hope, that forgets about the future, as it eats from the flesh pots of Egypt. The structure of oppression, accordingly, is able to create a man in its image and likeness, a man whose consciousness is as unfree as that of his master. He is the slave who does not want to be free. His will to freedom becomes will to domestication.

The history of freedom, therefore, cannot be based on the powers of man alone. If there is a history of freedom that negates the present and thereby creates the possibility of a new tomorrow, a history dependent on a power of freedom that transcends history and determines itself to be in and for history, it is because this power, God, does not allow the suffering of futurelessness to be dissolved in the oblivion of happiness in suffering. The slave may forget about his suffering, but God does not. God is the suffering God, the God who does not ever allow the pains of history to be overlooked and healed by the hypnotic power of the politics of preservation. Because God, as the presence of the future, is the God in history, and since his presence in history is always resisted by the powers of the old, God is a suffering God. There is no possible theodicy, no possible justification of what is by referring it to God. God is not the explanation of the pains of the world. On the contrary, he is the permanent power that denies the justice and right of suffering in history by being himself the God who suffers. He remains the Suffering Slave (*doulos*—Ph 2:7). How can history be explained, how can suffering be justified if God does not explain or justify it? He simply suffers. "The Bible," comments Bonhoeffer, "directs [man] to the powerless and suffering God. [He] is weak and powerless in the world, and that is exactly the way, the only way, in which he can be with us and help us."[19] It is only because God participates in the weakness and sufferings of the slave who forgets about his impotence and pain that there can be hope of liberation for him. The sufferings of God are thus the ground of hope for those who are without hope.

God therefore is to be found not among the powerful but among those who are subject, who suffer, who are not given a future. In the words of the Second Isaiah, the power of God is embodied in the most humble, most weak, most oppressed suffering servant. He looks "like a root out of the dry land, marred beyond human semblance." He had "no form nor comeliness and no beauty that we should desire him" (Is 52:14, 53:2). He does not shine with the glory of the tomorrow but bears the stamp of the pains of today. He cannot be otherwise, because he suffers with and for the people whom he loves. He bears the griefs and carries the sorrows of men (v. 4). Like the slave who is under those who have power, "he was oppressed," afflicted, like the lamb that is led to the slaughter (v. 7). He does not suffer because of masochistic tendencies. There is no glorification of suffering as something good. He suffers because he participates in the pains of those who are oppressed and without hope. It is the violence of those who hold power that makes him the "Suffering Servant." "His suffering has a super-personal meaning" because it is "God who suffers with him . . . for the redemption of the world."[20] The God about whom the language of the community of faith talks, consequently, shows a total partiality for the poor and oppressed of the earth (Ex 22:25). The sufferings of the poor and weak are his own sufferings. Accordingly, "he does not judge [men] for their iniquity against Him, but for their iniquity against each other."[21] The sufferings of the oppressed are thus not simply the sufferings of men but God's sufferings. "When ye are hostile to each other, ye hunt me down. When ye plot evil against each other, ye torment me. When ye slander each other, ye deny me. Each of you exiles his comrades and so together ye exile me. . . . Dream not that my forehead radiates heavenly beams. The glory has remained above. My face is that of the created being."[22] Buber's poetic way of expressing the biblical vision of God's identification with man's suffering sounds like a paraphrase of the same motif in the language of Jesus;

> *I was hungry and you gave me food;*
> *I was thirsty and you gave me drink;*
> *I was naked and you clothed me;*
> *I was sick and you visited me;*
> *I was in prison and you came to me.*
>
> (MATT 25:35, 36)

To the disciples' reply that they could not remember when that had happened, Jesus' explanation was that "as you did it to one of the least of these my brothers, you did it to me" (Matt 25:40). The "I" which is the subject really does not stand alone. It is rather the unity "I-they," in which the face of the "I" looks like the face of the "they." This identification is intrinsic to the historicity of God. The God who determines himself for history in this same act elects himself for participation in the sufferings of man. And only because of this can he help. The Christian community, consequently, came to identify the Suffering Servant with the Messiah: the One who suffers the sufferings of men is the One who has the passion, vision, and power of human liberation. The cross, then, which is fundamentally the symbol of the hopelessness and futurelessness that order and religion created, came to be seen as the beginning of a new possibility for history. If God suffers with and for man, man is assured that his personal negation of the negative in history is not a lonely voice. God himself negates it by his own suffering.

Because God suffers with and negates the unfreedom of today, it is possible to hope for a tomorrow in which man will be made free.

But the suffering God undergoes another type of suffering as well: he suffers when the slave should suffer but does not. The slave's inability to suffer is the result of his domestication. He has become ahistorical, unable to hope, impotent to think of a future in which he will become free. He is happy because of his alienation; he has become unable to feel pain when his historical situation of slavery is painful. His consciousness has become closed for the future. And when this happens "the time has arrived when man has become unable to give birth to a star" (Nietzsche). He has become barren and sterile, to the extent to which he has fallen prey to the power of the facts of the situation of slavery in which he is. God suffers, then, because man is no longer his companion in the politics of freedom. The pact between God and man, sealed because of their common vision of and passion for the future of liberation, is broken. God is alone. His suffering now is the suffering of loneliness. His politics of liberation had made man taste the first fruits of freedom, the "aperitif" of the new tomorrow. However, man has "unlearned hope," has forgotten the future, and has opted for the security of the present. He bows down to the idols. God's wife has become a harlot (Hosea 3:1), God's son has opted for a strange adventure of unfreedom (Luke 15:11-24).

But where man is unfaithful to the gift of the vocation for the future, God remains faithful. The language of the community of faith is the language of the faithfulness of God to his vision of and passion for human deliverance, in spite of the fact that man rebels against the future, and prefers rather the security of unfreedom. God's election of himself and of man for the future remains unshaken, even when man elects himself for the old. This is grace: the persistence of the presence of the future, even when man has become hypnotized by the power of the old. God's suffering is the negation of the negative of human consciousness; he does not allow it to pronounce the final verdict about the future of man and of history.

The cross embodies both forms of suffering. Christ suffers because of the violence of the political powers that close the present, and he suffers because of man's fear of the presence of the future. The cross stands thus between both the objective and the subjective rejection of hope. But the cross must not be understood as an isolated event. It is rather the culmination of the suffering that determined Christ's whole life. We must not think, therefore, that his death "is . . . the only thing that matters. [It] cannot be separated from his life."[23] He suffers, in his whole life, under the power of the legal and religious structures that make man unfree. And therefore, he finds himself identified with the victims of these powers: the outcasts, the prostitutes, the helpless, the poor, the sick, the lepers, the sinners, the enemy, the heretic. And he suffers, as well, because of all those whose consciousness is closed for the future and who, therefore, represent the powers of oppression. He finds himself, therefore, against those who embody the sacredness of political and religious structures.

If the subjective and objective powers that preserve man under bondage are those that make him suffer, "what is cannot be true."[24] If the God who is the presence of the future suffers with history, through his suffering he declares the inhumanity and falsity of the powers that dominate the present. This conclusion, however, for the language of faith, does not depend on the verdict of human consciousness. Its validity is absolute even when man has become unable to perceive it because of his domestication under slavery. The cross is not, consequently, either the absolutization or justification of suffering, or the announcement of the final triumph of the ambiguities in history.[25] It is a concrete negation of what is. "Hope finds in Christ not only a consolation in suffering," observes Molt-mann, "but also the protest of the divine promise against suffering."[26] By radically negating what is, on account of the suffering it causes, history is forced to look for a new tomorrow.

Suffering is thus the mother of hope. When it engenders the negation of what is, it prepares the way for a new day. It is historical suffering that keeps hope radically historical, as the overcoming of what today makes man unfree for the future and for life. If this were not so, hope would vanish in the indefiniteness of an abstract future and would be unable to serve man in his task of creating the new tomorrow.

The community of faith, consequently, came to see that in order to participate in the politics for a new tomorrow it is necessary to participate in the sufferings of today. The life of the community in the present is not, therefore, understood as a triumph, but rather as participation in the ongoing sufferings of Christ in and for the world.[27] Because God has elected himself for history and man, his sufferings will continue, with man and history, until the end of the world. What makes a Christian what he is, Bonhoeffer comments, is his "participation in the suffering of God in the life of the world."[28] The community of the future, therefore, does not discover its futuricity because of an esoteric knowledge of the world of the future, but rather from its identification with the sufferings of the slaves, the outcasts, the hopeless and futureless man, weak and impotent, the wretched of the earth. It is the Suffering Slave, who is present in the suffering of all the slaves in the world, who, from Christ's suffering, finds the secret of and the power for the liberation of man. "Only in the depths of suffering and despair," Buber states, "do men come to know grace."[29]

History, thus, moves toward the future through the suffering of the slave. It groans in travail. Only through its pains will the new man be born. The God of history, therefore, has not yet arrived. As man does, he lives in hope, awaiting an earthly consummation with man. To the extent that suffering remains, there is no reconciliation. God's ongoing suffering indicates his irreconciliation with what is and his commitment to its transformation. Reconciliation does not describe a reality. It belongs to the universe of the discourse of hope. It exists only as what is possible, through the freedom of the suffering God. "The so-called biblical center of reconciliation," remarks Dr. Christian Beker,

> may not be as central to the New Testament as recent theology has asserted. Reconciliation must pass through the revolution of the cross; and even apart from biblical insights, reconciliation may not be a target-word in our time since a bourgeois affluent Church interprets it inevitably as a sanctioning of the *status quo.* Reconciliation in the race issue has simply been translated as integration. Whereas the Church should have recognized that integration which bypasses "Black Power" demands means a resurrection without cross.[30]

It is true that the New Testament declares that we are reconciled with God (Rom 5:1), but only through our participation "in Christ," in his sufferings with and for the world. We are reconciled with God to the extent to which we share in his irreconciliation with a world that makes him and men suffer. This is why peace with God means a "sword" for the world—the permanent judgment and rejection of the untruth of what is, for the sake of a new tomorrow of reconciliation and liberation.[31]

The Politics of Liberation: The Historical Horizons Are Made Open for the Positive

The historical experience of liberation of the community of faith cannot be understood, therefore, as the natural unfolding of the possibilities immanent in history. From the politics of preservation of the old, the new could not evolve. Power does not give up power. Will to power does not become will to liberate. The domesticated consciousness of the happy slave does not evolve to will to freedom. The natural development of the historical process according to what is possible to it is nothing but variations on the motif "Masters-Slaves." It changes to the quantitatively different, but it is unable to negate itself in order to give birth to the new.

The event of liberation, therefore, implies the interruption of the normal course of history. History is negated, is resisted, is denied the right to follow the course it has determined for itself. But history is negated only to the extent to which the power that negates it is free from it. If it were not free from history it would be a child of history, a new embodiment of its will to power, a reflex of its structures of domination. Only what is free from history is able to oppose and transgress it. There is no liberation in history, no creation of the new, if there is no freedom and transcendence over the given subjective and objective conditions intrinsic to history. On the other side, however, there is no liberation if freedom from history does not determine itself as freedom for history. Freedom from history, by itself, is the negation of history but does not mean a new day for history. It was in the name of God's transcendence over history that theology, in many different ways, abdicated hope for the event of liberation in history. God's freedom would not be the beginning of a new day but rather the end, the radical and definitive No addressed to the whole of historical reality. The negation of history would not be for the sake of a new tomorrow in history but rather for the abdication of hope in history. It would imply that history was without hope and that hope lives only when it abandons history. The advent of the new in history, however, indicates the commitment of freedom to history. It is always freedom for history. Only as such does it become historical power that transcends both the objective structures of domination of the master, and the slave's will to domestication. The event of liberation indicates that a subversive power has been introduced into history, a power that negates and stops the old in order to make room for the creation of the new. Only when freedom becomes historical through power, through an activity that changes concretely the subjective and objective conditions of history, is the history of bondage brought to a stop, thereby giving birth to the possibility of liberation. Through this activity, transcendence comes to the midst of life. And only as such, as a reality in the midst of life, is transcendence an element of the language of the community of faith, as it is determined by the historical experience of liberation.

The starting point of this dialectical activity of negation of the old for the sake of the new, as we indicated previously, was the fact that God was the "Suffering Slave." The slave is the consciousness in history that can experience in the most painful form the inhumanity of history. He is the man without future, the man who does not have a right to hope. The condition of the slave, consequently, has in itself the secret of freedom. The master does not want to negate history. All his powers are dedicated to the task of its preservation. The slave, whether he is aware of this fact or not, is the negation of "what is," is a stretching toward the new. The secret of freedom which the condition of the slave contains is that "what is" must be negated for the sake of liberation.

Although the condition of the slave contains the secret of freedom, he does not always have the will and power to freedom. When the community of faith identified its God with the slave, it was thereby indicating that the secret of freedom which the condition of the slave contains is in God united with the will and power of liberation. Liberation does not stand or fall with man's consciousness and power. It is not something that depends on the powers of man alone. It is rather the sole determination of the God who is the Suffering Slave.

But in order to liberate the oppressed, the lamb must become a lion, the slave must become a warrior. The will to liberation expresses itself as power against those who make liberation impossible. Love for the oppressed is wrath against the oppressors. The process of liberation is thus the judgment on the master. In order to make the slave free, the objective powers and instruments of oppression must be destroyed. The instruments of the oppressor, his tools of domination, the yoke he puts on man's neck, the rod with which he hurts the slave (Is 9:4), the boots of the tramping warriors, the garments rolled in blood, the swords and spears of those who make war (Is 9:5, 11:4) have to be destroyed, to become fuel for the fire. God's power for the liberation of the slave exalts those of low degree and puts down the mighty from their thrones; it fills the hungry with good things and sends the rich away empty (Luke 1:51-53). The life of the Messiah, therefore, is a political conflict with the powers of domination. Because God lives in history "he does not fix history from the sphere of the yonder side and [from a sphere] strange to it," comments Buber. "He does not allow history to be unrolled as a scroll, but He Himself enters into it and conquers it in warfare."[32] The Messiah, consequently, is not "a spiritual 'anti-king' "; his business, liberation of men under bondage, gives to his activity and kingdom a political or rather 'theopolitical' character. The activity of the Messiah, therefore, is like entering a strong man's house in order to plunder his goods. In order to do this, however, the strong man must be tied up first and reduced to impotence (Matt 12:29). God's historicity, revelation, accordingly takes shape as power for salvation. And this means, in a first stage, power against the politics of the Antichrist, the politics of bondage. Through God's will to liberation the powers that keep the world in bondage—principalities, the world rulers of this present darkness, the spiritual hosts of wickedness (Eph 6:12)

—are reduced to nothing. God's presence in the world is like a bomb, to be set exactly under the powers of the old. They are to be objectively and subjectively exploded. God's politics, thus, is subversive of the stability created by the violence of the old. The false peace of unfreedom is put out of balance and its walls of defense are made to crumble.

There is violence involved in the process. God does not wait for the dragon to become a lamb. He knows that the dragon will rather devour the lamb. It must be opposed and defeated by the power of the lion. God does not wait for the warriors to come to the conclusion that peace would be desirable. He burns their weapons. He does not wait for the master to decide freely to liberate the slave. He knows that the master will never do that. So, he breaks the yoke, and the erstwhile master can no longer dominate. The power of God destroys what makes the world unfree. This use of power looks like violence because it destroys the equilibrium and peace of the systems of domination. But, as we indicated before, this peace is really the triumph of the violence of oppression. Thus, what looks like the violence of the lion is really the power of counter-violence, that is, power used against those who generate, support, and defend the violence of a world of masters and slaves. Violence is power that oppresses and makes man unfree. Counter-violence is power that breaks the old which enslaves, in order to make man free. Violence is power aimed at paralysis. Counter-violence is power aimed at making man free for experimentation.

The use of violence is in the politics of the Messiah an instrument to liberate even the master against whom it is used. The lion snatches from his hands the sword and yoke, the instruments that defended him against the future. He is forced, unwillingly, to confront the reality of history and of the future. He sees the past and present pass by. He is then thrust into the sphere of "holy insecurity" and confronted with a new possibility of revelation, of a new self-understanding. He is forced to see the clay feet of his idols. And when the idols crumble, they lose their grasp over the master.

The politics of liberation, however, not only explodes the political powers of bondage. It is directed against all the powers and structures that make man unfree for the future, for history. It is

possible to see this dynamics in operation in the process of secularization, whereby man is being forced again out of the womb of
religion, of meta-historical certainties, back to the provisional horizons of history. The politics of God directs its attack against the
Tower of Babel and against the Temple, as structures that separate
man from a historical future.

The "happy slave," with the disruption of the structures that
kept him safely under bondage (be the bondage political or religious oppression, or any other kind of power that makes man
unfree for the future), is forced to come of age. He is no longer
under tutelage. He is forced to be free and to face the responsibilities implicit in the task of building the earth.

Seen within this context, it becomes obvious that love cannot
be a principle for behavior. When love is transformed into a principle, it is disconnected from the historical dialectics of the politics
of liberation, which is the only form in which love really exists.
Love describes the identification of the Suffering Slave with the lot
of the oppressed, it points to the liberating direction of his activity.
It cannot, however, become a snapshot of what he does. To transform love into a principle is to dehistorize it, to transform it into
a "dogmatic idea." From the point of view of the historical experience of the community of faith, love is the name for the dialectics
of liberation in history. Love is what God does in order to make
man free. Because our ways of theological thinking have, to a great
degree, overlooked the historical and dialectical contents of the
language of the community of faith, the language of love, instead
of being a help for the understanding of the politics of liberation in
the world, has rather become a problem. The use of power came
to be seen, not as the expression of love, but rather as a concession
that love makes to the contingencies and imperfections of historical
life. From the perspective of dialectics, however, since the man
who is afraid of the future is unable to liberate himself, love takes
shape as an activity that aims at the destruction of the objective and
subjective conditions of slavery. This is the dark side of the politics
of liberation: the "No," love as power against, wrath against, the
oppressors, the *opus alienum Dei.* It is a No, but nevertheless, it
remains a work of love, as activity for the liberation of both masters

and slaves, because through the destruction of the objective and subjective structures intended to forestall the future they are forced to move toward the future. They are made free from the past, to the extent to which the past, through this activity, loses its political and hypnotic power over them.

But the *opus alienum Dei* is done for the sake of the *opus proprium Dei*, the No for the sake of the Yes, the destruction for the sake of the building up, the liberation from the past for the sake of the liberation for the future. The despair that follows the destruction of the idols is followed by hope and expectation, since the activity that breaks down the old promises something new. "Remember not the former things, nor consider the things of old," says the Liberator. "Behold, I am doing a new thing." "I make you hear new things, hidden things which you have not known. They are created now, not long ago" (Is 43:15-19; 48:6-7). The politics of liberation announces therefore that, as the result of God's messianic activity "the old has passed away and a new thing has come" (2 Cor 5:17). The normal unfolding of the politics of the old cannot give birth to the new. The new is here nothing more than the old under a different form, a different mask. It regenerates itself, thereby perpetuating the old world of unfreedom under a different guise. But because God's politics negates the natural unfolding of the old, room is made for the new. And one can truly say that it is created *ex nihilo*, since the new cannot be explained in terms of the logic of natural causality. A new subject emerges in history: the master and the happy slave are no longer the same. The man who was once the object of history, impotent, the suffering slave, becomes now a subject. He is made free to insert his freedom into history in order to build a new tomorrow according to his love and creativity. But more than that: the face of the earth can now be changed. It is free to become a new earth, a site of recovery, no longer under the hold of the will to power that made it hostile to man.

It seems that it is within this context that the language of the resurrection of Christ becomes meaningful. It is ironical that the language which for the first Christians was the expression of freedom has become for us today rather a problem to be solved. It has become a problem because we have come to live in a time in which nature is taken as the limit of history. The idea of the resurrection, which is basically that of freedom recreating nature, cannot, therefore, find a place among the other phenomena dealt with by normal historical science. We do not have factual analogies that could provide the categories needed to set the fact of the resurrection among other historical facts. But at the same time we cannot simply ignore the absolutely central place that the resurrection had in the language of faith, since it was part of the historical experiences that shaped the early Christian community. The way out of the impasse, it was and has been argued, is to internalize the language of the resurrection. It would not have any rapport with objective history, objective time, objective structures. The resurrection would refer to the sphere of subjectivity, where freedom is possible. It would stand for a new self-understanding, the liberation of the self made free from the past, from the fear of death, for the future. The resurrection would accordingly have a place in the universe of discourse of subjective freedom. Obviously this means that the resurrection is not a valid category for objective history. This history remains determined and limited by causality and unfreedom. The event of freedom or the event of the resurrection would thus mean that man is lifted up from history. He finds hope and liberation to the extent to which he is no longer determined by the objective structures of history. Resurrection means thus, at the same time, hope without history and history without hope. Borrowing from Kant his separation between the world of causality and the world of freedom, we rescued the idea of the resurrection from obsolescence by making it an event of *Geschichte*, the existential history, whereas *Historie* remained untouched by it. This split made possible a great contradiction: to be both revolutionary in the subjective world and conformist and conservative in the objective world; to speak the language of freedom in the domains of the existential and at the same time to speak the language of calculation in the sphere of politics and science.

It seems, however, that the universe of discourse of biblical messianism does not allow for this separation. Within its context, the subjective hope is derived from and dependent upon what God does objectively in history. It is because God makes the future open that consciousness is made open. There is no room for fictionism: man does not hope as if the future were open, while knowing objectively that the future is closed. God gives hope because he gives a future (Jer 29:11). Biblical messianism is, thus, a different way of understanding history, derived from the historical experiences with the God of liberation. When history is seen as the history of freedom, of the ongoing politics of freedom as it opens the way towards liberation, nature cannot be seen as the limit of freedom; it is exactly the other way around: freedom is the limit of nature. That this was so for the community of faith is obvious from the fact that the idea of creation was, for it, an afterthought, totally determined by the historical experiences of liberation. The God who makes history is the God who created the world. Creation, consequently, was not understood as a category of nature but as a category of history. It was *creatio ex nihilo*, the gift of God's determination to create a future. The idea of creation is thus part of the same language of the resurrection that sees freedom as what determines the subjective and objective possibilities of history.

If this idea of the informing, life-giving, future-directed power of freedom is of such central importance for biblical messianism, it seems that it is in this context that we should understand the function of the language of the resurrection for the community of faith. This obviously means that we will be missing the point if we understand resurrection simply in subjective terms, because this would imply that freedom is unable to shape history. We also would miss its meaning if we take it as simple fact, as an objective, finished event, because from one fact we cannot generalize to the universal activity of the power of liberation in history.

It seems that the New Testament references to the resurrection do not describe it simply as a given fact. Resurrection is rather part of the universe of the discourse of faith. The "appearances of the Lord" do not occur outside the event of faith. One does not exist without the other. The appearances of the Lord were, therefore, an experience of his power. It meant to have the same Spirit which raised him from the dead (Rom 8:11), to be liberated from fear (Rom 8:15) and to live in the glorious liberty of the children of God (Rom 8:21). Language about the resurrection does not, therefore, treat it as fact that can be dealt with objectively outside the context of this new freedom.

But the other side must be emphasized, as well. The resurrection is not identified with and exhausted by this new self-understanding. On the contrary, it implies the unity between the subjective and the objective. It indicates that the same Spirit which makes man open for the future is making objective history and creation free. Thus, man's freedom and hope are related to objective possibilities of liberation in the world of time and space. At least this is the way Paul understands it. The Spirit which raised Jesus from the dead, which made us free for the future, is the Spirit which made the whole creation pregnant. Creation, too, hopes, unconsciously; it "groans in travail," in the expectation of its own redemption (Rom 8:19-23). And its movement toward the future is not only determined by the same Spirit which raised Jesus from the dead but is parallel with and concurrent to the movement of human liberation that goes on in history (Rom 8:21): creation will be set free from its bondage . . . and obtain the glorious liberty of the children of God! When Paul again discusses the import of the resurrection in I Cor 15, he relates it to the triumph of freedom over the powers that objectively keep man captive, the last of which is death (vv. 24-26). The resurrection, therefore, does not describe either an objective fact in isolation, or a subjective event in isolation. It points to the unity of both, to freedom's power over history, and therefore to the possibility of hope from, in, and for history.

The word resurrection, in the universe of discourse of the community of faith, does not describe, therefore, an organic process. It does not indicate either that a dead body was brought to life again or how it happened. As Moltmann indicates, there is a gap between the cross and the resurrection. The One who was dead was experienced by the community of faith as alive again. But nothing is said about the "how," about what came in between. Resurrection, like creation, was an expression of freedom's power to create *ex nihilo*, to give life to the dead and to call into existence the things that do not exist (Rom 4:17). The word was borrowed from Jewish apocalypticism to express the community's experience that the One who had been crucified was alive in history, as a power of liberation. Through this language Jesus could no longer be referred to simply as a fact of history, finished, plunged in the past, in the sphere of what had already happened. He could not be described in biographical terms. He was not a *fact*, simply, but rather the *factor* of history, the power of freedom that creates the facts of liberation. Jesus was now historically experienced as an informing power in history. But as a factor he did not simply happen; he was happening. As a fact, one could describe Jesus as a man who had been free; resurrected, he was experienced as the One who was making history free. Resurrection meant accordingly that the Suffering Slave, the One who had the secret and power of human liberation, was making history free. He is, therefore, the Lord of history. The cross thus becomes the central point for the understanding of the possibilities of liberation in history, not as the total relativization of all directions and options, but rather as the power which, in every situation, negates the power of what is, in order to make possible the creation of the new. The resurrected was thus "the life-giving spirit" (I Cor 15:45), One who was making men and the world alive again for hope and for the future. The resurrection does not, therefore, express the final fact about God, because it is not an arrival point. God did not arrive at his goal through it. He is an ongoing God, and the resurrection describes his ongoing activity that, through the negation of the Suffering Slave, liberates history for the future.

Resurrection, hence, is the language of the ongoing politics of God in history. It is the language of hope. It points to what we can expect. "In this hope we were saved," Paul states (Rom 8:24). As hope, it cannot be verified by handling the events that became past. The past events can be the "aperitif"; they do not, however, offer any ground for verification. This is why no historical research is able to "verify" the resurrection. It could verify a fact, but not a factor. The field of the verification of hope is not, therefore, the past, but the future. Hope is verified to the extent to which man is made open for the future, the structures of oppression are broken, and the future is made open for man. And each of these events is a new celebration of hope, a new enjoying of the "aperitif" of liberation.

The language of resurrection, therefore, refers to what we can expect from history, as being penetrated, liberated, made alive by God's freedom for history. It points to the possibility of the event of the *novum,* of the creation of the new. In this context it is possible to hope. To live in the light of the resurrection is to live in eschatological tension, in the expectation of the event of the new subject and of the new tomorrow. But it must be said that resurrection is radically opposed to any type of triumphalism, because the power of the resurrection is the dynamics of the cross. Therefore, man is compelled to participate in God's sufferings in the world. Wherever man is being oppressed and destroyed, there God is being crucified and killed. But in the context of hope, suffering loses its power to draw man to despair, and becomes the fertilizing No from which the powers of bondage are destroyed for the sake of a new tomorrow of liberation.

CHAPTER FIVE

THE GIFT OF FREEDOM:
MAN'S FREEDOM FOR LIFE

The discussion of the vocation, historicity, and dialectics of freedom could give the impression that freedom is the dominating noun of the language of messianic humanism. This is not, however, the case. From its historical experience freedom is always determined for man, it is instrumental of the human. In its language, therefore, freedom plays the role of the verbs, of the judgment, of the movement, whereas the nouns and adjectives point to the life which the dynamics of freedom gives to man. One does not have any meaning without the other. Freedom, as simply freedom from, would be the negation of life. It would not be power to fertilize, to create the new, to give life. Life, in turn, outside the context of freedom, would make man similar to an animal, the prisoner of organic time, as he is in the religions of nature. The unity of freedom and life in one and the same universe of discourse indicates that life, to be human, must be historical, determined by freedom; and that freedom, to be human, must be the bearer and giver of life.

The biblical community expressed this idea through the concept of the pact. As we indicated above, that community's historical experience was that both the reality of its liberation and the gift of the land and it fruits were to be seen not as the result of their power to be free as a people, but rather as the gifts of the politics of liberation in which they were caught up. Both their movement and the enjoyment of the good things of life were understood as having been made possible by the fact that there was a pact, a bond of faithfulness that united them with the power which was making history free. They did not, however, enter into an agreement of the *do ut des* type. Quite the contrary: they were recipients and as such their freedom and the whole content of their life was a gift of grace. Life in freedom, and freedom in life: this was the project of the dynamics of the politics of God. Freedom in life and life in freedom were thus to be found as the community moved in faith and trust in the loving power of the Suffering Slave, on the one hand, and in responsible obedience to his ongoing politics of liberation, on the other. Participation in the politics of God produced, therefore, the reality of freedom for life. The signs of God's activity, consequently, came to be understood as the signs of the human. God's freedom for man is historically visible as it makes possible man's freedom for life. This way of relating God's freedom for man and man's freedom for life was suggested by Bonhoeffer through his image of the polyphony of life.[1] Where the ground bass, God's politics of liberation, is firm and clear, life explodes in a polyphonic melody in which all earthly affections, worldly pleasures and joys find their truth and autonomy. One does not have any reality without the other; but neither can they be confused.[2] The language of freedom, therefore, does not swallow up the nouns for the sake of the verbs, but rather sees the verbs and nouns as related in such a way that they cannot be separated without thereby destroying both of them. Freedom and life are brought together in such a way that the "flesh" of God's freedom for man is man's freedom for life. The movement of the language of freedom, therefore, turns our eyes to the gift it promises and brings: life, with all its fullness, its joys, its goodness.

Man's Freedom for the Future

This freedom for life is made possible because in the context of God's politics the future loses its threatening aspects. When the future is the symbol of death, a threat that will destroy man and that must, by all means, be avoided, life ceases to be life and becomes the living presence of death. Abandonment and joy in life are impossible because the life man loves so much is what carries within itself the death that will destroy him. The future, therefore, cannot be the occasion of liberation, if it is feared as the possibility of the end. In the context of trust and faith in God's loving, liberating politics, however, the future is transfigured. It ceases to be the occasion of threat and becomes the object of joyful anticipation. It is no longer the time when man will lose himself, but rather the time that will bring new possibilities of being authentically free and alive. Man's mind experiences *metanoia.* It is no longer determined by the powers of bondage and death that paralyzed, but rather by its experience with the power of resurrection which "gives life to the dead and calls into existence the things that do not exist." It functions according to the "mercies of God" (Rom 12:1) which make the future the bearer of a new possibility of life. Man's life has shifted from a backward to a forward look. He is free because freedom, as Bultmann points out, "is nothing else than being open for the genuine future, letting one's self be determined by the future."[3]

The new orientation of man's consciousness means a new direction for his action. The man who is afraid of the future acts in order to prevent the future from happening, through the neurotic affirmation of the present in which he is preserved as he is. If man, on the contrary, is open and determined for the future, his action becomes midwifery. It is intended to help history give birth to the new tomorrow which now makes it groan, suffer, and hope as does a woman in the pains of childbirth. In the first case man fears, therefore he acts. In the context of the politics of God, man hopes and therefore he acts. His action is the child of his hope and bears the marks of his love and freedom for a new future. The language of hope, as the language of that which is possible to history, from the perspective of God's politics of human liberation, then becomes an intrinsic part of ethics, as the science and activity that aims at the historization of hope.

If man acts because he hopes, it becomes obvious that the yes is ultimate in human action. Man negates only for the sake of the new which is to be affirmed. His hope-oriented activity is thus to bring to fulfillment the positive that was hidden in the activity which negated what made man suffer.

Hope implies that man is made free from the past, as from a prison. This is not to say that the past is forgotten, but rather that it ceases to be the dominating factor in human behavior. Man remembers the past and is grateful for it, but his memory of it makes him aware of an ongoing politics. The past, therefore, cannot exhaust the possibilities of human life. Man is thus made free from the "photoelectric" style of life that always reads backwards and makes man unable to move (Lehmann). The future, and not the past, is where the liberating possibility for the today is to be found. This means that man is free from the ethics of law and principles, which imply a mistrust in man's freedom and responsibility since they rigidly limit the unfolding of the polyphony of life in the future. The past sets the pattern for the future. As law and principles cling to already established values that supposedly provide the structure of the future, they bring experimentation to an end. They refuse to allow man to take the risk of a new future. In the context of messianic humanism, however, human freedom finds as its point of reference an ongoing politics of liberation that pushes toward the future and makes possible the expectation and welcoming of the new and the boldness to act in ways not foreseen in the past.

If action is the midwife of the future, then human activity can add the new to the world. It can indeed be an act of creation. God's grace, instead of making human creativity superfluous or impossible, is therefore the politics that makes it possible and necessary. This is so because in the context of the politics of human liberation man encounters a God who remains open, who has not yet arrived, who is determined and helped by human activity. God needs man for the creation of his future. "If God did not need man," remarks Friedmann, "if man were simply dependent and nothing else, there would be no meaning to man's life in the world. 'The world is not divine sport, it is divine destiny.' "[4] The creation of the new future is thus part of the mutual pact of faithfulness to the liberation of man that unites God and man. As God's freedom was apprehended by the community of faith from the activity that made freedom and life possible, so man's freedom is to become a praxis, an activity that makes the world different. Man's freedom, therefore, is not only a dimension of his subjectivity; it is power to transform the world, to create a new future.

Man's creative activity is thus the instrument through which he recreates and recovers nature. Before being penetrated by man's freedom, nature was perhaps a "thing" together with man in the impersonal world of contacts, which was an instrument for his domination by the masters. Nature was either alien and impersonal, or hostile and aggressive. Human creativity can, however, give it a new face. Creativity is the activity through which the existential, man's passion and hopes, become external in the object thus being created. Man creates the world in his own image. He is even able to have communion—and not mere contact—with this world because it is no longer a brute fact, but rather a world fertilized and transformed by man's sweat and creativity. It becomes, consequently, the mirror in which man can see the reflections of himself and his neighbor. Nature is thereby humanized, historized. Through man's creativity there is hope for the earth which can be transformed into a home and a site of recovery for mankind.

But it is not only nature that is recreated through man's activity. Man himself becomes different in the process. His action is to create a new future, it is to express his love for a new tomorrow. The new tomorrow, however, can only be built from today. Efficacy in the creation of the new is impossible if action does not take as its point of departure the concrete possibilities the present offers. The love for the new tomorrow and the exigency for efficacy demand, therefore, man's permanent openness to his present world. He remembers his past experience. He probes his world. He relates his memory and experiments to the need for action in his now. He makes choices, takes risks, makes mistakes, retreats, reorganizes his action and, with it, himself. In and through this interplay with history he changes and becomes different. He becomes as open and future-oriented as the historical context within which he finds himself. He discovers that he is not a monad but rather a horizon. He is experimentation. The negation and hope and consequently the action they inform cannot, therefore, be defined a priori since they are extracted from and are a response to man's understanding of what it takes to be and to make the world human, from and in his concrete historical context. This is why "humanization is not . . . a process which can be foreseen in its totality and through which we become more and more similar to an idea of man," Esdras B. Costa comments. "It is rather an experiment in which the criteria of humanity are discovered and transcended by other better criteria, and applied to life by free men and women, in their faithfulness to their vocation of human beings."[5]

We mentioned that freedom for the future is liberation from the future as a threatening possibility. This freedom takes on flesh, however, only when we understand it in the context of this possibility of creating a new earth. When man's hope informs his action, man thrusts himself upon the world as power. He wants to overcome, through his negation, what makes man suffer, and to create a new tomorrow, according to the hope extracted from the negation. In all relationships of power, however, there is a risk involved. To stand over against a given reality as power is to be resisted by it, through power. Man discovers that the world is not then simply there, passive like a piece of marble, ready to be given a new form. The world reacts because of the political powers involved in its present form. It resists man. It becomes threatening. Man therefore consciously takes the risk of being defeated. He takes the risk of death. However, because of his hope that through his risk the world may yet be transformed into a site of recovery, man accepts the possibility of death for the sake of the world.

The full meaning of this new freedom for death is understood when we compare it with a different way of approaching the same problem as suggested by Heidegger. Man, he indicates, is existentially a being-toward-death. He knows that he exists now but that in the future will no longer live. To the extent that his existence is conditioned by his fear of death, his life is nothing more than death in life. Fear makes him unfree to be what he is ontologically called to be. He betrays the call of his conscience to a life of freedom and becomes dominated by defensiveness. How could he become free for life? Only by having the courage to be free for death, to accept it as the limit of his existence, when he ceases to fight against its approaching reality. Freedom for life is found in freedom for death. Norman O. Brown offers a similar interpretation of the problem. Commenting on the meaning of Christian hope for the resurrection of the body, he indicates that what it really implies is that the body must be reconciled with death. To accept death is the precondition for the liberation of the body for the possibilities given to it. He then adds that Christian theology "must either accept death as part of life or abandon the body."[6] As with Heidegger, the acceptance of death is the precondition, the beginning of the resurrection of the body for the life of freedom which it could have.

In the context of the politics of God, however, the solution assumes a different form. The primary fact is not that of death but rather of life. Man is made free for life, and therefore remains stubbornly irreconciled with death as the *fact-or* of history. Such irreconciliation is what makes man willing to take freely the risk of the fact of death, knowing that exactly in this act his freedom for life triumphs over the power of death. He finds his authentic life not by accepting death through a purely formal or subjective decision but rather as willing-to-be-toward-death-for-the-sake-of-the-world. Death becomes a risk that has to be freely taken in order to make it possible for the world to become a site of recovery for man. He comes to know, then, literally, that he who keeps his life, loses it, and that he who willingly risks losing his life, finds it (Matt 10:39). The triumph of life over death, therefore, does not come as the result of man's reconciliation with it. This triumph emerges rather from his irreconcilliation with death, which, from his love for life, takes shape as willing-to-be-toward-death-for-the-sake-of-the-world which is to be recreated for the sake of man and his life. The difference introduced here becomes clear by the use of a simple example. A woman does not will to give birth to a child because she understands and accepts the possibility of dying in the act. Just the other way around: only because she loves and is therefore determined for the sake of the child is she willing to face death freely. It is not freedom for death that makes man free for love and sacrificial action, but it is rather his love for his suffering fellow men who need to be liberated that makes him ready for the risk of death involved in sacrificial action. "When a woman is in travail," said Jesus, explaining his freedom for death, "she has sorrow because her hour has come; but when she is delivered of the child, she no longer remembers the anguish, for joy that a child is born into the world" (John 26:21). The anguish and sorrow implied in the struggle for a new world are thus caught up in the joyful anticipation of the dawning of a new day. As the fear of death freezes freedom by creating an ethics of defense and survival which orients activity toward self-preservation, so the confidence in the future which the Messiah promises makes man free to express his love in freedom from calculation. "Through Jesus Christ, through his life, death, resurrection, and reign in power," H. R. Niebuhr remarks, "we have been led and are being led to . . . the reinterpretation of all our interpretations of life and death. Death no less than life appears to us as an act of mercy. The ethics of death is replaced by the ethics of life, of the open future, of the open society."[7]

The participation in this adventure of creating a new tomorrow is thus of higher importance because it is related to the possibility of an authentic life, free from the domination of death. Authentic life cannot be separated from the objective possibility of transforming the earth. Marx's analysis of the tragedy of the worker is curiously close to what we have noted. The worker's tragedy, he observed, is not based on the fact that he is a worker or that he is poor, but rather on the fact that he is set within a structure of production that separates him from the world. His existential dimension is separated from the objective. His creativity is unable to create the earth. What he does is not creation but rather alienated labor, toil that is not an instrument by means of which the worker penetrates, fertilizes, and changes his world. He produces something but this thing stands over against him. He does not contribute to bring about a new tomorrow but rather to the perpetuation of his today. At the end of the process the worker is not made richer through self-expression; there is no room for that. He is rather poorer because he has lost part of his life without communicating to the world something of himself. "The work . . . is not part of [the worker's] nature; he does not fulfill himself but rather denies himself through his work. The worker, therefore, feels at home only during his leisure time. His work is not a satisfaction of a need, but only a means for satisfying other needs."[8] The act of creating (which in his case is not really a creation) then becomes a burden. His life is found outside work; work, therefore, is what threatens life. It is a form of asceticism, a discipline to which the worker has to submit himself in order to be able to enjoy what really matters to him. The act of work is thus radically a negation of the body and of life, death-in-life. The worker is then led to believe mistakenly that freedom for life is liberation from work, leisure, free time for the enjoyment of something else for which labor only provides the economic means. It seems that this is the ideal that the prophets of the cyber-cultural era are proclaiming as the liberating gift of automation and guaranteed income: freedom from work, from toil and starvation, from anxiety about one's future economic security, time made free for what is really important for man. This solution, however, which is precisely what the alienated worker dreamed of, does not eliminate the basic alienation but rather perpetuates it. Man's creativity still remains impotent to create his world. In the first case he could not create the world because his power was absorbed by those who owned the means of production. Now he cannot create history because his power is no longer needed by those who own the means of production. In the first case, the owners were those who determined the direction of history; now it is the techno-bureaucratic elites who determine the shape of the future.

The problem of humanization, therefore, is not to be understood as liberation from labor, which means the perpetuation of the split between the subjective, the existential, on the one hand, and the objective world of things and structures, on the other. The task is rather related to freedom for labor and to the liberation of labor, so that it will be the means whereby man brings his freedom, his love, his determination for life to bear upon the earth in which he lives in such a way that it will become a new earth.

Humanistic messianism thus sees the solution with great clarity: only as the creator of history does man find his authentic life; only when man is the creator of history is there hope for the world.

The above reflections show how similar messianic humanism is to humanistic messianism—and how different. Humanistic messianism believes, with messianic humanism, that man's vocation is to create history, in one way or another. But against messianic humanism, which acts because it hopes, humanistic messianism hopes because it acts: liberation is to be achieved by the powers of man alone.

Protestant theology, it seems, has provided a radical critique of all movements that are dominated by this messianic obsession about what man can do through his activity. Historically, that theology began as a protest against man's illusions about his own powers, and the anxiety, fear, and frustration to which they led. In order to liberate man from the burden of creating his own salvation, Protestantism proclaimed what is absolutely central for messianic humanism: that humanization is primarily a gift of grace, that man is free to relax because his future is not his business only. Protestant theology declared that in the context of God's grace the future cannot be the cause of man's anxiety but rather the object of his joyful expectation. It started thus as an expression of that passion for human liberation by the powers of the Messiah which make man free from both the anxiety and the messianic obsession caused by his illusion as to his responsibilities and possibilities.

The rest of this insight, however, was strange. Since Protestant theology believed that the only possibility for the liberation of man from both his messianic obsessions about his power to make himself free, and from the anxiety and fear that inevitably followed, it concluded that there was no room for human creativity in history. Grace, accordingly, instead of making man free for creativity, makes creativity superfluous or impossible. Work is therefore not a tool to be used in creating the new, but rather an expression of obedience to the command of the One who was the only creator. This trend becomes evident in a number of instances. It appears in Luther, in his interpretation of work as the discipline of the monastery brought to the center of life, as mortification, and *preparatio mortis.* In Calvinism, according to Weber, this trend plays a crucial role. Work is the expression of the "intra-worldly asceticism" whereby man dominates the world in order to demonstrate historically his eternal election. In Harnack work reaches its lowest point, as it is seen as nothing more than "a valuable safety valve" which is "useful in keeping off greater ills"[9] but totally separated from man's spirit. Barth's theology does not provide a reevaluation of the import of work. It follows the line traced by the Reformation. Because what God does exhausts the possibilities of history, work becomes "an incidental but necessary prerequisite of his service," "a fulfillment of the law of the human nature," "a movement within the created world," in short, "play." "For this reason," Barth remarks, "a participation in it can have nothing to do with participation in the work of God."[10] Grace does not make creativity possible; it renders it unnecessary. Consequently man remains commanded to move but made unable to create. No wonder that humanistic messianism finds itself opposed to Protestant theology. Its theology of work is almost a theology (or ideology) of alienated labor, that is, the justification of labor that does not create the new.

Messianic humanism, from its historical experience, finds it necessary to preserve both grace and creativity. It therefore rejects both the messianism that believes that liberation is created by the powers of man alone and the Protestant destruction of work as the instrument for the creation of history. And as it does this it preserves the critical element of Protestantism and the creative thrust of humanistic messianism. How is this possible? In the context of God's politics of human liberation grace creates the possibility and necessity of man's action. Man is a co-creator. The pact between God and man means that God waits for what man can give to the new tomorrow. The pact means that God, in the fulness of his eternity, needs, longs, and waits for man. "There is something essential that must come from man" in God's future, Friedmann comments. He "awaits an earthly consummation, a consummation in and with mankind."[11] Within God's politics "man's action is enclosed in God's action. The one is no less real than the other and neither is a part cause."[12] In this context the words of the apostle which otherwise could sound so confusing acquire a new meaning: "Work out your own salvation with fear and trembling; for God is at work in you, both to will and to work for his good pleasure" (Ph 2:13f.).

The autonomy of human activity which is the ground of the hope of humanistic humanism is rejected. But the isolation of a God who makes history without men, who moves ahead alone and self-sufficient, perhaps a God who has already arrived, is rejected too. Salvation is achieved through a politics in which God makes man free to create. Creation, therefore, is still unfinished. It is ahead of man, as a horizon which is made free over and over again, and which offers itself to man as an invitation. "We may imagine perhaps that creation was finished long ago," Teilhard de Chardin writes. "This is not true. It continues more graciously than ever . . . and we serve to complete it, even with the humblest work of our hands. . . . In each of our works we labor, in a very minute but real way, to build the Pleroma. . . . In action I adhere to the creative power of God; I coincide with it."[13] In a true sense man is really helping God when, for love for his fellow man and inspired by the vision of a new earth, he becomes involved through his actions in the task of transforming the world of today into the new earth of tomorrow.[14]

If creation is a joint enterprise, the God who is involved in the politics of liberation remains open. He does not look at history from his future nor does he pull history from his future. In history, with man, their future is engendered. This is so because the future is created historically with man. It is not simply a future created by God for man, but by God and man, in historical dialogical co-operation. This is the necessary implication of his incarnation: that he remains open to man. But openness implies unfinishedness, it implies that one still is in an experimental stage. The incarnation of God means thus that he remains historical and is adding to himself everything that is human. In the Messiah all the things in heaven and earth are recovered and united (Eph 1:10). "God can no longer do without the many among whom he has immersed himself," observes Chardin, and therefore, even what seems to be lost is taken up again by God. His incarnation cannot thus become a "take off" point from which God builds an ontological reality separated from what is going on here and now. He remains historical. He has not yet arrived.

From this perspective history is the history of freedom. It is indeed an ongoing process of political nature which makes the present free for the future and man free for life. The focus of attention is not what has become past but the future that can be created. In this ongoing process of creation and re-creation God's creativity brackets man's creativity. It is a joint enterprise in which creator and co-creator, together, build a new future. If this is history, man's historicity cannot thus be understood simply in terms of his ability to understand, remember, relive, to interpret history but rather in terms of his vocation and power to co-operate in the creation of a new tomorrow. We conclude, with Marx: "The philosophers have only interpreted the world in various ways; the point, however, is to change it."[15]

Man's Freedom for the Present

We observed above that the language of the community of faith is marked by a profound sensibility to the tragic sense of life. The centrality of suffering is such that it is not referred to simply as a reality of the world and history, but rather as a dimension of God. He was the Suffering Servant. This tragic sense of life was later translated by the Christian Church into a thrust toward asceticism. If God suffers because of the world, the world, for the sake of God, is to be negated, and there is no more certain way to achieve this negation than by transforming the world into a thorn that makes man suffer. This extrapolation, however, is totally absent in the language of the biblical community. We never find there this conjunction of the tragic sense of life and asceticism. On the contrary, the Old Testament especially is full of a tremendous taste for life, an exaltation of the world of senses, and a freedom to find joy in the good things that life gives man. How is it possible to explain the conjunction of these two elements, the tragic sense of life and the taste for life? Christian thinkers and preachers became used to the explanation that the biblical communities could have joy in spite of the world, because their faith related them to an other-worldly reality in which suffering was overcome. They experienced, accordingly, a sort of spiritual joy that exists in conjunction with suffering. Psychologically, the community of faith could be classified as dominated by masochism, since its suffering was the occasion for its joy. The problem with this interpretation is not only related to its inhumanity but to the fact that the language of the community of faith tells a totally different story. It speaks about love for life, for this world, not a joy beyond life and the world. Its objects and occasions are very worldly: the bread that strengthens man's heart, the oil that makes his face to shine, the good wine that makes him glad (Ps 104:15), the bodily presence of a friend, the pleasure of sex, the relaxation of rest. This is joy in the world and in the present, because of the world and because of the present. It is a language that overflows with the Dionysian erotic sense of life and never apologizes for it. The words uttered by the Creator in the myth of creation are, really, the same words the community addressed to the world, in the joy of enjoyment: "It is very good!"

There is, however, a fundamental difference between the enjoyment of the world found in the community of faith and the same phenomenon as it occurs in the religions of nature. For the religions of nature, nature was the giver of life and therefore to be both enjoyed and respected as the sacred limit for man. Enjoyment here requires adaptation, domestication. Man exists within and for the sake of nature. It was otherwise with the community of faith. Its experience with nature was conditioned by its vision of history, of the liberating freedom as it opened its way toward a new future. Consequently, nature was experienced as the gift of the freedom that determines itself for the sake of man. The idea of creation therefore does not convey a cosmologic theory but rather an historical perception of the for-the-sake-of-man character of the earth and everything that exists. The politics of liberation, the politics of agape, which moves ahead in spite of man, produces and gives to man a reality that has a beauty, a joy, a permission of its own, and which makes eros possible and necessary. Man cannot express his gratitude for God's gift except through the joyful and erotic acceptance of the gift. The *telos* of agape is thus eros. It cannot be otherwise. Protestant theology has been absolutely determined to maintain the centrality of agape. This word describes the "God for man," the Messiah who graciously liberates man, in spite of man's resistance and impotence. With this option Protestant theology has taken its stand decisively on the side of history. However, if agape fills the horizon, if the language is dominated by the verb, we will be dangerously bordering on a gnostic way of looking at the world, which would never have anything in itself worth being loved. Love would be always "in spite of." If the dynamics of agape are taken seriously, one must also take eros seriously. Perhaps we should recover the truth of Aquinas' affirmation that "God loves all existing things, for all existing things, insofar as they exist, are good,"[16] as a needed element in the reconstruction of creation and its erotic import as part of man's freedom for life.

Because the good gift of the earth is for the sake of man, a noun in the language of the community of faith acquires a central importance: body. It is only through his body that man is able to receive the gift. Man's body is what establishes his solidarity with the world and the world's solidarity with him. Through the body man discovers himself as a child of the earth. He is made "of dust from the ground" (Gen 2:7). Nature is his body, and therefore his bread. This is why nature is that "with which he must remain in a continuous interchange in order not to die."[17] Through his body he discovers nature as his body. It is not, therefore, an alien entity. It is friendly, caressing, a place of joy and happiness, his home. Through his bodily senses man is able to have delight in nature. He finds himself in a garden, a place of aesthetic enjoyment. A garden is a combination of colors, shapes, smells, movements, rhythms, sounds. In a garden the sensorial possibilities of man are stimulated to the utmost. He is forced out of reflection upon himself, and becomes open like a horizon for that which comes to him, from outside. That world which was there, outside, through man's body becomes a part of himself. But more than that, the body is what mediates between man's existential dimension, his freedom and love, and the world that invites him. Through his body he is able to fertilize and transform the world through his work. It is the body, therefore, that enables man to receive the gift as something for the sake of his creativity. The gift then assumes another aspect: it is given, it is there, enjoying a solidity and autonomy of its own. Man can take it, break it, explore it. He is then able, because of his body, which relates him with the given gift, to build a science of nature, because the gift does not have holes, empty spaces within which God hides himself. Man may confidently explore nature as something really given. And through his body, man thinks. He does not pluck out his eyes in order to see better. His thought requires the senses. He does not generate the object from the thought, but the thought from the object. He gives names, and as he gives them he is not simply creating symbols for the objective but rather expressing the relationship between the objective and himself. The name describes his perception of the world, as something there for the sake of himself, the world as a gift.[18]

His body is what makes him a person. "The body alone is that negating, limiting, concentrating, circumscribing force, without which no personality is conceivable. Personality, individuality, consciousness, without nature, is nothing."[19] Through the body man discovers himself as a person, as individuality, and only through it the sense of over-againstness and singularity is created. This means that the body is the precondition of communion. Through the body man reaches the consciousness of himself as an "I" in the experience of meeting the other body, the "Thou" which is over against him. Through the body man discovers therefore that he does not exist as a monad. He receives his being from the "Other." He is social. He is sexual. His body drives him to the other. He is not attracted primarily by agape, namely, love for the other in spite of what the other is. It is eros that drives man to the woman and woman to man. Manhood and womanhood: this is part of the goodness of creation and a reality that conditions and makes necessary the erotic sense of life. The abstract self at which the philosopher can arrive by means of abstraction, the primal center of consciousness which is not bodily conditioned, bodily determined, and dependent upon the body, has no reality for the biblical taste for life. Indeed, it is when he discovers the other that man recognizes the world as gift. Feuerbach observes:

> Without the other men, the world would be for me not only dead and empty, but meaningless. Only through his fellow does man become clear to himself and self-conscious; but only when I am clear to myself does the world become clear to me. ... A man existing absolutely alone would lose himself without

any sense of his individuality in the ocean of Nature; he would neither comprehend himself as man nor Nature as nature. . . . The sense of Nature, which opens to us the consciousness of the world as a world . . . first arises through the distinction of man from himself.[20]

The perception of nature as a gift of freedom to man is thus mediated through man's discovery of freedom through love and communion with his fellow man. Moreover, it is through this communion and the freedom it implies that man discovers historical time. Without freedom man is simply immersed in nature, he is part of it. Through communion he discovers will, the power to project, his transcendence over nature. Spirit is therefore a dimension of the body, "the power of futurity"[21] that determines the body. This is why the language of the community of faith definitely opposes the platonic negation of the body. The future of man is in the resurrection of the body.

One does not find in this language, consequently, any place for transcendence beyond the world or beyond the body. Man's liberation has to do not with the negation but rather with the liberation of the body from everything that represses it, makes it unfree for the world or the world unfree for it. We are confronted here with the most materialistic of all religions, William Temple comments.[22] It is not, evidently, physical materialism of the type inaugurated by Democritus which ultimately reduces everything to the play of atoms, but rather a vision of the material world, the earth, the body, the senses, as the creation and expression of freedom, and as the only means through which freedom carries on its politics of liberation. The Messiah, the power of liberating freedom, is "flesh." There is no room for a God who gives himself to man or who operates outside the material conditions of life. There is no room in the Garden of Eden for a temple. God is found amid the things he gives to man. Luther was deeply aware of this element of the language of the community of faith. God's freedom for man, he indicated, takes objective, concrete form in the world. This was a conclusion he derived from his Christology. If God determined himself to be always for man, in and through a bodily form, it was necessary to speak about the omnipresence, the ubiquity of the body of Christ, filling the whole universe. The body of Christ "must be essentially present at all places, even in the tiniest tree leaf, . . . in every single creature, in its innermost and outermost being, on all sides, through and through, below and above, before and behind, so that nothing can be more truly present and within all creatures than God himself and his power."[23]

We do not have here a cosmic interpretation of Christ, a "cosmic Christ," but rather a christological interpretation of the cosmos, the cosmos as seen from the perspective of the messianic history of liberation, a "Christic cosmos." Transcendence, therefore, is the deepest dimension of the world of visible things in which we live. Baillie interpreted Luther's vision of transcendence as "mediate immediacy,"[24] God's presence in and through the visible and sensorial. The sensorial thus is not a springboard that catapults our thoughts beyond the sensorial, in search of the God who has created but who does not give himself in and through creation, as he is conceived in Thomist theology. The sensorial is not simply an instrument, a *via*, a way that leads us to the world of eternity, but rather the locus, the only place, the only form in which we meet transcendence. This is why in Luther it is possible to find a deep taste for life and appreciation for the goodness of all created things which, through the historical consciousness of the community of faith, can and must be accepted as the erotic creation of God's agape. A similar language is spoken by Teilhard de Chardin: "Christ gives Himself to us through the world which is to be consummated in relation to Him. By means of all created things, without exception, the divine assails us, penetrates us and moulds us. We imagined it as distant and inaccessible, whereas in fact we live steeped in its burning layers." As we meet the cosmos we are really facing the "universal Smile" which creates that "taste for being," because through the world, "being . . . became, in some way, tangible and savorous" to us.[25]

The body and the cosmos thus become, as they are seen in the perspective of the history of freedom, the occasion for an erotic exuberance, the possibility of the triumph of the Dionysian over the Apollonian style of life, the permission for that overflow of vitality, enjoyment, pleasure, and joy in and through the life of the senses.

The gift is very good. One cannot receive it without feeling its delicious taste in the mouth, the taste that whets the appetite for more: the gift is the "aperitif" that makes man happy, but does not make him drunk in his happiness. He longs for more, for fulfillment, for the resurrection of the body, for the fulness of life of which our present situation is only an exhilarating foretaste.

It is because life is so good, the body so full of possibilities, the world so inviting, that suffering is so painful. Suffering emerges as one experiences the repression imposed upon life, which neither allows man's body to be free for the world or the world to be free for man. Suffering emerges as a result of, and as a protest against, whatever, in our present historical reality, makes the fulfillment of the erotic sense of life impossible and therefore aborts the project of agape, of the politics of the Messiah. Suffering does not, therefore, spring either from subjective morbidity or from a pessimistic assessment of the world and its possibilities. One suffers when one sees that the sprouts that promise that spring is coming are killed by the return of winter. One suffers because the explosion of joyful expectation created by the "aperitif" is frustrated by the powers that keep man under repression. A protest song, written by a Brazilian poet, expresses beautifully how suffering springs from this erotic sense of life.

> *As two and two are four*
> *I know that it is worth while living,*
> *Although bread is scare*
> *And freedom too little.*
> *As your eyes are light*
> *And your skin tanned,*
> *As blue is the ocean*
> *And calm the lagoon,*
> *As the night carries the day on its lap,*
> *From beyond terror*
> *A new time of joy waves to me.*
> *As two and two are four,*
> *I know that it is worth while living.*[26]

The light eyes, the tanned skin, the blue ocean, and the calm lagoon, the night that carries the day on its lap: this is the "aperitif" that, in the today of repression, suffering, scarce bread, little freedom and much terror, creates the erotic taste for life and the longing for a new tomorrow of liberation. It is the permanence of this joy, in spite of suffering, that keeps alive the vision and hope for a new time of joy. The dialectic is not, therefore, between a present that is totally negative, and to be negated as a totality, and a future that ideally eliminates this suffering, thereby becoming pure positivity. This would be a new form of docetism that totally negates the present for the sake of the future. Suffering and negation exist historically only because of and for the sake of the liberation of the good and joyful the world presents to man. "One can believe in the resurrection and a new world," Bonhoeffer comments, only when "one loves life and the world so much that without them everything would be gone."[27]

Humanistic messianism, like messianic humanism, is definitely committed to the liberation of the body. It starts with the body; in the name of the body it negates whatever makes the body suffer, whatever means violence and repression, whatever causes hunger and death. It is for the sake of the body that it hopes for a new tomorrow in which repression will be brought to an end. And it is through the body that it plans to liberate man for the world and the world for man. It is for the sake of the body that it has rejected religion. Feuerbach found it necessary to "de-theologize" the Christian faith in order to recover the true object of religious language, man. And the elimination of God meant, basically, the liberation of man from the non-sensorial world, the world of metaphysical ideas and realities, and his liberation for the world in which he had his true being, the world of the senses and of nature. The words with which he ends *The Essence of Christianity* are the summary of his understanding of what it takes for man to be human. "Therefore, let bread be sacred for us, let wine be sacred, and also let water be sacred! Amen."[28] Through the dissolution of religion he proclaims man's freedom for nature and nature's freedom for man. The same note is struck again in the writings of Nietzsche. He inveighs against Christianity because he sees in it the total negation of the life of senses, of the body, of the world, for the sake of God. Christianity is a "hatred against everything human, animal, material," "a disgust with the senses," a "fear of happiness and beauty," a "will to nothingness . . . which runs counter to life, a revolt against the most fundamental presuppositions of life."[29] In order to make room for God, Christianity has to kill man. The attack against the anti-body powers takes a different form in Marx. The enemy is private property, on which he writes:

> Private property has made us so stupid and partial that an object is only ours when we have it, when it exists for us as capital or when it is directly eaten, drunk, worn, inhabited, etc., in short, utilized in some way. Thus all the physical and intellectual senses have been replaced by the simple alienation of all these senses; the sense of having. . . . The less you eat, drink, buy books, go to the theatre or to balls, or to the public house, and the less you think, love, theorize, sing, paint, fence, etc., the more you will be able to save and the greater will become your treasure which neither moth nor rust will corrupt —your capital. The less you are, the less you express your life, the more you have, the greater is your alienated life.[30]

The domination of the sense of having is, therefore, the total alienation of life, since it represses the erotic sense of life and sublimates it through the power of ownership.

The passion for and vision of human liberation of humanistic messianism and messianic humanism, thus, converge in one point: both hope for the resurrection of the body, the resurrection of nature, the elimination of repression, the triumph of the erotic sense of life. Norman O. Brown summarizes very well the future that is hoped for:

> The question confronting mankind is the abolition of repression—in traditional Christian language, the resurrection of the body. The resurrection of the body is a social project facing mankind as a whole, and it will become a practical political problem when the statesmen of the world are called upon to deliver happiness instead of power.[31]

Although the repression of the body and the fear of the erotic may express themselves as a dimension of subjectivity, it would be a mistake to think that the social project of the resurrection of body could be achieved through the therapeutic processes of psychiatry or any other process of individual liberation. We must not forget that repression assumes political and economic form, as structures, powers of repression. The problem, therefore, is not only the subjectivity which is unfree for life but rather the total articulation of repression that makes the expression of the erotic sense of life impossible, even if man is subjectively free for it. That is why Marx criticized Feuerbach sharply for believing that the simple fact of unmasking subjective illusion would bring about the needed liberation. The same criticism can be directed against Norman O. Brown. What is necessary, therefore, is a praxis that liberates society from the structures of repression.

Messianic humanism is deeply conscious of this fact. The liberation of the erotic sense of life is a gift of the messianic politics of liberation. It is, therefore, restored to man only as he participates in God's politics through suffering, negation, hope, and obedient action.

The community of faith finds itself consequently in a permanent conflict with the erotic sense of life of the conservative, because it never occurs "on the way." For the conservative, his enjoyment of life is the end of history. As he drinks life he carefully eliminates from his cup everything bitter. He becomes unable to suffer with those who suffer. His own enjoyment makes him drunk and occupies the whole horizon of his concerns. He therefore wants to eliminate everything that challenges his enjoyment of life. He is unable to see that his enjoyment is both a contradiction in the world and a cause of the contradiction of the world. It is a contradiction in the world because it willingly ignores the pains of those who are poor and weak. It is a cause of the contradiction of the world because in order to maintain the level of enjoyment of its society, exploitation and oppression of those from whom it can derive more affluence and more security are required and justified. His enjoyment thus gives birth to structures of repression that either destroy the body of man or make the good things of the earth inaccessible to him. The erotic sense of life of the conservative loses its spirit, its character of "aperitif," its future orientation. Instead of making man more eager to bring about new forms of freedom for life in the world, it becomes the instrument for his domestication. He becomes fat and unable to move.

In the context of the God's messianic politics of liberation the erotic sense of life exists only as it keeps man open for a new future. Life is there, to be eaten, but man is to eat it with bitter herbs, with his loins girt, his sandals on his feet, and he shall eat it in a haste (see Ex 12:8–11). The bitter taste of suffering can never be eliminated from the "aperitif", so that man will never settle for it.

But messianic humanism also rejects the opposite sin of the revolutionaries. Since the revolutionary believes that the elimination of repression and the restoration of the erotic sense of life depends on the powers of man alone, he finds it necessary totally to discipline his present in order to gather his energies for the task of liberation. In order to destroy the repression imposed upon society he finds it necessary to impose upon his present a similar structure of repression. The present loses itself. It exists only for the sake of a future. It is a time of transition, a time of asceticism. The future—not the present—is the time of the liberation of the erotic sense of life from repression. The present accordingly becomes the absolute negative. And the future to be liberated by revolutionary action, on the contrary, becomes the absolute positive. As metaphysics and religion denied the earth for the sake of heaven, the present is here denied for the sake of the future. Man is absolved from inhumanity and brutality in the present, as the time of transition, the time which does not count. And the future, once it is brought about by the revolutionaries, tends to become closed, because it is believed that it is the presence of the "eschaton." This is why revolutions that were once the bearers of new hopes soon became crystallized, rigid, and dogmatic, a veritable resurrection of the sins of the conservative. On the other hand, if the project of liberation by the powers of man alone fails, man does not find ways to survive in the presence of captivity. The flame of the taste for life is extinguished by frustration and bitterness. It was in a similar mood that a poet wrote Psalm 137:

> *By the waters of Babylon*
> *there we sat down and wept*
> *when we remembered Zion.*
> *On the willows there we hung up our lyres . . .*
> *O daughter of Babylon, you devastator!*
> *Happy shall he be who requites you with what you*
> *have done to us.*
> *Happy shall he be who takes your little ones and*
> *dashes them against the rock.*

This is the song of the absence of the future, the absence of joy, of lost time, of the time only of suffering; time against man; the time of the end of man.

But more than this: the liberation of the erotic sense of life by the powers of man alone implies that only those who have power to actualize it will have something to hope for. Those who are weak, sick, blind, unable to enjoy sex, those who remain captive of the fear of the world—these remain as marginals, as abnormalities for whom the language of the erotic sense of life cannot have any meaning. The new society is, really, a new type of elitism, the society for the strong, healthy, and beautiful.

The community of faith, however, does not find the erotic sense of life at the end of the praxis of liberation, but rather in the midst of it. On the way toward the new tomorrow man receives the gift of the present, the time of enjoyment, the time that does not exist for the sake of any other time. There is a time of rest, of contemplation, of pure joy. On the way toward the promised land man learned that there is a time when he has to stop, to abdicate all attempts to build the future, to remain in pure receptivity and in a total abandonment of calculation. His today was God's gift. He could rest because the politics of liberation was not carried on by the power of man alone, but rather by the passion and activity of God. Therefore, it was not only possible to rest in the present without losing the future but rather necessary to rest in the present in order not to lose the future. In the New Testament we find the same thing. The One who is recognized as the presence of the future and who acts in order to bring about the future is exactly the One who commands the acceptance of today in total abandonment and liberation from anxiety:

> Do not be anxious for your life, What you shall eat or what you shall drink, nor about your body, what you shall put on. Look at the birds of the air. . . . Consider the lilies of the field. . . . Do not be anxious about tomorrow. Seek first his kingdom and his righteousness and all these things shall be yours as well (Matt 6:25-33).

In the context of the politics of the kingdom man thus discovers that the whole world lies open before him as a gift for his enjoyment. Man is then made free to be like a child who accepts today in a total liberation from anxiety about tomorrow. Man is free for the simple things of life, things that will not make headlines or change the world. Free to chat, to drink and eat, to remain inactive in pure contemplation, to enjoy the sex game, to play. He is liberated for humor, which exists only when man does not take himself too seriously, when he is not dominated by messianic obsessions about his power to create history. He is free for a joke, for art, for the contemplation of nature. Because man's life is bracketed by God's politics, which makes today open for a new tomorrow, the present becomes free for man. It really is a good gift to be accepted and enjoyed with thanksgiving. Man is free even to live in captivity, without either losing the erotic sense of life because of the frustration of a future made closed, or without becoming drunk by eroticism as a compensation for the loss of the future. This, it seems, is the meaning of the letter of Jeremiah to the captives in Babylon:

> Build houses and live in them; plant gardens and eat their produce. Take wives and have sons and daughters; take wives for your sons, and give your daughters to marriage, that they may bear sons and daughters . . . (Jer 29:5-6).

What more terrible advice could the prophet give to the revolutionaries? How could they plant trees and wait for their fruit? How could they build houses in the land of captivity and live therein? Moreover, how could they wait for the birth of their grandchildren? The fact, however, is that for the prophet even the time of captivity is the time when it is possible to remain human, provided one is neither dominated by the bitterness of despair, the loss of hope and of the erotic sense of life, nor domesticated by the flesh pots of captivity that create the happy slave, the erotic enjoyment of life that makes hope impossible. In captivity one remains human only as one who "hopes against hope." But this is possible only in the context of trust in the politics of God that makes even the time of captivity the time of pregnancy for a new tomorrow, the time to which "a new future and a hope" are given (Jer 29:11). In this context man finds freedom from the obsession for freedom (Hoekendijk). Here, the social project of the resurrection of the body ceases to be only a hope given to those who are strong and alive and becomes the universal project of the resurrection of the dead: the universal liberation of the body for the erotic sense of life in a world given to man for his enjoyment and happiness.

CHAPTER SIX

THEOLOGY AS A LANGUAGE
OF FREEDOM

We began these theological reflections by asking about the possibility of a new language of faith that could express the vision of and passion for human liberation. We indicated that the need for this new language was derived from the concrete commitment of many Christians to the task of making man historically free from the powers that keep him in bondage. We pointed out, moreover, that amid this process Christians were being confronted by the language of political humanism which criticizes radically, on good grounds, any language that speaks about "theos," any theological language. We believe that this encounter provides the occasion for the death and resurrection of both the language of faith and the language of political humanism. This is what we attempted to indicate in the preceding chapters.

It seems possible at this point to present a summary of the main elements of this new language of faith which has been the object of our exploration.

1. It is a totally historical language. Its verbs and nouns speak together about revelation as history. Its verbs describe and point to the political dialectics that created in the past (and therefore makes possible to hope for) the event of human liberation from bondage. Its nouns, in their turn, do not refer to meta-historical objects. On the contrary, they have the solidity, colors, smells, and shapes of earthly things. They refer to the good world which, as the *gift* of

the dialects of liberation, is over and over again penetrated, re-created, and resurrected by the activity of freedom. They speak about the sufferings, joys, and hopes of man. It is therefore a human language which rejects everything that does not refer to the world of man and which incorporates in its universe of discourse every-thing that refers to man's world and hope of liberation. Paraphras-ing Feuerbach: the language of faith "unconditionally repudiates absolute, immaterial, self-sufficing speculation—that speculation which draws its material from within."

Those who speak this language differ totally from those "who pluck out their eyes that they may see better"; for their way of speaking requires "the senses, especially sight"; it finds its "ideas in materials which can be appropriated only through the activity of the senses." It does not "generate the object from the thought, but the thought from the object." Its "ideas" are not self-subsistent entities; they are only "faith in a historical future."[1] It does not, therefore, draw its nourishment and strength from the holes, bor-ders, or corners of human life. The word "God" is not thus "a stop-gap for the incompleteness of our knowledge."[2] If this were the case theological language would be like a parasite whose strength would be directly proportional to its ability to exploit man's weakness. Where man is tormented by guilt, there it would speak about forgiveness, where man is afraid of death, there it would utter the word life, where man is in despair, there it would say "hope." There is no way of defending this language against Freud's charge that it is nothing more than "wish-fulfillment."[3] The language of faith, as a language determined by and for history, does not speak about a meta-historical, meta-worldly realm in which hopes are fulfilled and sufferings are brought to an end. It remains historical through and through, both in its verbs and nouns, and it is within this historical and earthly context and content that it speaks about the reality and possibility of human liberation, about the reality and possibility of freedom for life.

2. The fact that the intention of this language is historical human liberation indicates that the language, as such, has only a secondary import. The primary element from which it is born and to which it points is the ongoing politics of freedom within which

freedom for the future and freedom for life are to be found. It has a radically prophetic import. When the prophets said "Thus saith the Lord" they were simply "explaining God's intention and meaning in the events of their day."[4] It is within and because of the events charged with the liberating dynamics of freedom that man finds his humanity. The historical events, therefore, were the revelation and power of God's will. "The Word leads us not away from history, but to history and to responsible participation within history."[5] Language is thus nothing more, but nothing less than a footnote to the events which, in any specific moment, provided the vector and thrust of the possibilities of human liberation amid history. It does not, therefore, mediate a transcendental reality to man but rather provides a critical reading of the "newspapers," thereby inviting, nay, commanding man to responsible participation in the arena of history. This secondary, footnote function of language is of the greatest importance for our understanding of how past, present, and future are articulated in its universe of discourse.

The past brings to the community of faith the memory of what was once accomplished by the politics of liberation. When "the prophet looks backwards," Minear comments, "the story of the past becomes a parable and a sign of God's continuing purpose."[6] To remember the past is therefore to see what is possible to the present, within the perspective of the ongoing movement of freedom. Man is therefore sent back to his present, confronted with the provisionality of the powers which make man captive today, and the future, consequently, becomes open for hope. The past, therefore, is never a screen. It does not provide any excuse for the photoelectric language that has as its purpose to keep the past alive in the present, as if this were possible. Because the memory of the community of faith remembers a past of freedom, it thereby makes the community free from the past. The freedom about which its past speaks can not have been exhausted by the past, otherwise it would no longer be freedom in the present. It remains as the fact-or of history. "The past always is mediated," R. Kroner observes. "It is no longer life, but only the image of former life."[7] The past, when it was present, was the arena for the politics of freedom. But once it became past, it no longer could contain freedom. The past lies

finished, definitely beyond the grasp of freedom which is the presence of the future in the time that is now the today. The language
of the community of faith therefore totally ignores the problem as
to how to become contemporaneous with the fulfilled time of the
past revelation. It ignores both the problem and the possibility of
transtemporalization, that has been so central for Protestant
theology. Contemporaneity cannot be a problem for a language
that speaks about God as the presence of the future.

"Remembering the promise issued aforetime," Moltmann remarks, "means asking about the future in the past." The memory
of the community of faith is therefore "futuricizing." It is obvious
that the ability to hope for the future is not a monopoly of those who
have the memory of the community of faith. The power to project
is intrinsic to the will. It is an intrinsic expression of the spirit of
man. This power of transcendence over the hypnotizing grasp of
the given facts of the present, however, can be nothing more than
wish fulfillment or the source of utopian dogmatic plans of a perfect
society. For the language of faith the power to project is controlled
by the memory of the historical dialectics of liberation. It is the
language of hope as that which is possible to history and its future.
The future and the hope about which it speaks remain, therefore,
radically historical. As memory is prophecy in reverse, hope is
memory projected to the future.[8]

Past and future do not stand, however, as abstract dimensions
of time. They are respectively remembered and hoped for from and
for the sake of a concrete historical present. It is only when man
feels the pains and contradictions of the present and is committed
to its liberation that his past acquires the determination for-the-sake-
of-the-present and brings to it, therefore, a new dimension of negation and a new possibility of hope. It is only in the subject which
is inserted in its present that "past and future are welded into one
on the forge of life, with its ties and loyalties of man to man."[9] The
present is the time when man is alive, suffers, and feels joy. It is the
occasion in which negation and hope can become history through
the obedient action of man. The pains and joys of the present are
thus the elements that keep the past open, never allowing it to
become a screen, and force man to hope for a new future. The

welding of past and future, therefore, occurs only in and through the engaged intelligence which has the concrete historical conditions of the present as its permanent point of reference, for whose sake the whole process of thought is undertaken. "The verdict of the past is always an oracle," Nietzsche observes. However, "only as architects of the future, as knowers of the present, will you understand it."[10] The acts of remembering and hoping that determine the language of the community of faith, therefore, do not have any reality in themselves but in the engagement in the ongoing politics of liberation which is the situation and condition of theological intelligibility, that is, the situation and condition within which the language can be spoken.

3. When the community of faith speaks, it is expressing a historical experience in which no present is final. Its engaged intelligence suffers with the pains of the present, which indicates the element of untruth in it. When it remembers, it is confronted with a story of an ongoing politics of liberation which, in order to liberate the good gifts of the present in a new tomorrow, from what represses them today, has to be negative. This memory, although it does not create a critical attitude towards the present (which is only derived from one's insertion into its pains), informs both this critical attitude towards the present and the hope for a new future. The presence of the repressive and negative powers of the politics of preservation indicates thus that, *although revelation is history, history is not revelation.* It is not a divine process. The language of the community of faith, therefore, does not explain or interpret the riddle of history from the vantage point of a transcendental point of reference. It does not transform "facts into values."[11] On the contrary, it is expressive of the permanent negation and hope that relativizes and desacralizes every present.

If the language of the community of faith is, on the one hand, totally historical but, on the other hand, does not refer to history as a divine process, it is a language expressive of a secular world. A secular world means two things. First, it is totally historical. It does not look for metahistorical points of reference or values to organize itself. It "does not look behind the stars first in order to find a meaning for the earth." History is the horizon within which it moves. The language of the community of faith is therefore expressive of man's courage and determination to remain historical. And second, a secular world is an experimental world, a world that does not have a navel, a world that leaves behind possibilities which are negated and marches toward horizons which are still open. It lives in a constant elimination of absolutes because all absolutes are idols. The language of the community of faith is thus both secular and secularizing. Its secularizing import is derived from the secularizing direction of the vector of the politics of God. Only by remaining secular will history never become prey of the past. Only by remaining secular will every new tomorrow remain as a new point of departure, a permanent experiment, a constant exploration of new possibilities.

The language of the community of faith, therefore, as expressive of a history always being secularized, does not point to any eternal, absolute kernel in the midst of history. It is a language that floats in the ever-changing flux of history. One could ask if this language does not really express the end of man! Does not man need a glimpse of eternity and stability in order to survive? Does he not need the emotional experience with the "wholly other," with the "eternal now," or the knowledge of absolute truths in order not to be swallowed up by temporality? The answer that the language of the community of faith provides is that the permanent, the eternal now, the absolute in time, these are the real enemies of man that destroy his spirit. Transcendence in the midst of life takes shape exactly in the permanent relativizing of the present that makes it open for possibilities now arrested. Transcendence triumphs when all absolutes disappear and when man has to live in the "holy insecurity" of a totally secular world. But secularization does not mean profanity. A profane world is a world void of transcendence, separated from and opposed to it. When this happens man can never come to terms with this world and accept it as his home. In the context of the politics of God, however, the world is secular because of the secularizing impetus of freedom in its midst. Secularization is thus the positive creation of the politics of liberation. The dialectics of the politics of liberation and the secular world thus go side by side. Man is, consequently, free from the concern about absolutes, about religion, about the immovable, and free to live as a permanent experiment. This is why the language of the community of faith is in a permanent struggle against secularism. Secularism is a change of idols: the abandonment of metaphysical, religious, ecclesiastical absolutes, and the election of historical absolutes. This absolutization of history is described by Leszek Kolakowski in the essay "The Priest and the Jester": "A rain of gods is falling from the sky on the funeral rites of the one God who has outlived himself. The atheists have their saints, and the blasphemers are erecting chapels."[12]

This "desire for the absolute" is what creates the "secular priest" who absolutizes a new historical order or situation. It gives birth to priesthood, as a historical and political category. "Priesthood is not merely the cult of the past as seen through contemporary eyes," Kolakowski states, "but the survival of the past in unchanged shape. It is thus not only a certain intellectual attitude toward the world but, indeed, a form of the world's existence, namely, a factual continuation of a reality which no longer exists."[13] Historical idols do not cease to be idols by being historical. Their character of idols is derived from their power to forestall the future, to transform a certain historical expression into the navel of the world. They are idols because they are the presence of the past that does not allow the future and the new to take form in history.

The language of the community of faith, consequently, is iconoclast by nature. It shares not only in that "attitude of negative vigilance in the face of any absolute" of the philosophy of the jester, advocated by Kolakowski, but in its humor, which desacralizes by ridicule the comical pretensions of the "priests."[14] And those who speak the language of faith with the spirit of the jester must not forget that there is no humor when one is not ready to laugh off one's own voice. The iconoclastic, subversive, and humorous character of the language of faith, however, springs from the participation of the subject or community that speaks it in the ongoing politics that expresses the passion for and vision of human deliverance. It keeps its secondary character, its quality of footnote, its permanent reference to the "praxis," which mediates to history a new possibility of human life.

4. The language of the community of faith, consequently, is an expression of imagination. It is not purely descriptive. A purely descriptive language transforms facts into values. Imagination, by rejecting the facts as its limit, expresses reason's transcendence over the given. Imagination is a form of critique of what is, an expression of negation, a function of reason that is dependent on man's spirit, on his power to move beyond the closed world of the facts. A purely descriptive language is able only to name the things that are present and thereby sets them as the limit for man's freedom. A language created by imagination is able to "name the things that are absent," and when it does this it breaks the spell of the things that are present.

Both the scientist and the political humanist could, however, raise the question as to whether this language of imagination is not a form of alienation. There is no way of proving scientifically the truth of this language, they could claim. Everything indicates that it is not verifiable, that it is not falsifiable and that consequently it is meaningless, a sort of fictionism not willing to come to terms with the facts as they are. That might very well be. In every historical commitment to a thing that is absent a risk is involved. But, let me ask: is it not through a risk for something still absent that the language of science is able to open new ways towards the future? Does it not operate in a manner in many ways similar to that of the language of faith? Thomas S. Kuhn indicates in his book *The Structure of Scientific Revolutions*[15] that it is a mistake to believe that scientific discovery occurs by a simple process of accumulation of facts objectively described, without the aid of imagination. Kuhn suggests that the game of science is like trying to put together all the pieces of a gigantic puzzle, without having, however, the pattern of the whole. The putting together of the pieces is possible only because imagination, starting from some clues offered by some isolated pieces, is able to suggest an operative pattern, a paradigm which will, for a while, provide the rules for the whole game. Scientific theories are not arrived at by simply adding the facts, but rather by a creative leap of imagination that suggests the possible pattern for the many pieces still scattered. At the beginning, therefore, the scientist has no factual guarantee that his guess is right. He hopes, he believes. He does not move ahead with objective proof to support him. Verification thus, even for science, does not lie in the past but rather in the future. It is only when the scientist is able to take the risk of faith in his imagination, and to proceed as if the model provided by it were true, that he is able to verify the adequacy of his paradigm. After proceeding for a while with a certain paradigm the scientist will find out that many pieces do not fit in the pattern. According to his paradigm, these pieces are anomalies. He has then to put his imagination to work again in the attempt to find a new paradigm that will both integrate past gains and open the road towards new gains. Science does not move ahead, thus, by simply adding facts. Imagination is required. But imagination does not run wild, without any limits. It functions only when it takes with absolute seriousness the clues that the facts provide.

Imagination, in the language of faith, functions in a similar way. It offers paradigms that are supposed to open the way towards the future. Because its object is the future, as with science, only the future is the field of verification. The difference between the language of science and the language of faith does not lie in the fact that one can be proved whereas the other cannot, but rather in the fact that science is verified by the power of its language to put together the given pieces of a game. It operates exclusively within the limits of the given. The language of faith, on the contrary, is radically critical. It does not accept facts as values. It wants to destroy the facts that enslave man and to create new facts, now absent, that could make man free. Whereas scientific reason only describes, theological reason wants to create. The verification of the language of the community of faith is thus related to its ability to make man free for life, free for the future, free to negate the old and to create the new, free to remain free in oppositon to the untruth of the facts that do not make room for freedom. However, as it happened with the language of science, this function is possible only when imagination remains inserted into the facts, as engaged intelligence *(intelligence engagée)*. It is only as imagination remains inserted into the facts that the hope it is able to think remains as an expression of what is possible to history. The transformation of history according to hope is possible, thus, only when imagination remains faithful to the earth, to the concrete objective and subjective conditions of the historical present.

The historical character of the language of faith and its possibility of being verifiable mean, necessarily, that it can be falsifiable. There are historical situations that could prove that we totally misread and misunderstood the possibilities of history and consequently that our assessment of the conditions and power for human liberation is totally mistaken. The field of verification and the criteria of falsifiability are related to man's freedom for history and history's freedom for man. If history becomes definitely closed for man or man definitely closed for the future, if repression becomes the ultimate fact and domestication the ultimate determination of man's subjectivity, then we can say that the language of freedom no longer can be spoken.

The language of freedom, therefore, always runs the risk of losing itself. But this is the only way of being faithful to our condition as human beings, and the unavoidable risk involved in the adventure of faith.

NOTES TO CHAPTER ONE

1. Gerhard Ebeling, *The Nature of Faith* (Philadelphia: Fortress Press, 1961), 187.

2. S. M. Lipset and S. S. Wolin, eds., *The Berkeley Student Revolt: Facts and Interpretations* (Garden City, N.Y.: Doubleday & Co., Anchor Books, 1965), 213, 219.

3. *Ibid.*, 219.

4. Pierre Furter, "Caminhos e Descaminhos de uma Politica da Juventude," in *Paz e Terra* (Rio de Janeiro: Editora Civilizacao Brasileira), n. 3, pp. 27–28.

5. Mario Savio, in Lipset and Wolin, *Berkeley Student Revolt*, 217.

6. "The societies to which dialogue, true communication, is denied, and instead 'communicated things or results' are offered,—results of coercion and 'donation'—become preponderantly "mute." Muteness is not properly the absence of an answer. It is an answer void of critical content." Paulo Freire, *Educacao como Pratica da Liberdade* (Rio de Janeiro: Editora Civilizacao Brasileira, 1967), 69.

7. "From Paris, from London, from Amsterdam we would utter the word 'Parthenon! Brotherhood!' and somewhere in Africa or Asia lips would open '. . . thenon! . . . therhood!' It was the golden age." J. P. Sartre, in his preface to Frantz Fanon's *The Wretched of the Earth* (New York: Grove Press, 1968), 7.

8. The relation between "mutism" and impotence for action which creates the new is not to be found only among the poverty stricken people, because these are not symptoms primarily of economic deprivation but rather of a consciousness which is oppressed, which has not emerged into history and which takes the world as it is. Thus the young American student of the fifties presents the same symptoms of ahistoricity. He "wants very little because he has so much . . . and is unwilling to risk what he has. He is old before his time; almost middle-aged in his teens (from a Gallup poll). The college student was typically a professionally oriented young man, looking almost single-mindedly for a place which would *keep* him, and from which place, he was told, he might fall if he 'took chances.' He kept his mouth shut and his eye on the main chance; he aspired only to perhaps a better place in the manner to which he was born or to which

his father had so recently and with much sweat ascended." This generation "will bear the rubric of Silent Generation," and "helplessness may be the key" for its understanding. Notice the relation between silence, helplessness, and action directed toward the given. Lipset and Wolin, *Berkeley Student Revolt*, 385–386.

9. Sartre, Preface to *The Wretched of the Earth*, 15.

10. Cf. Fanon, *The Wretched of the Earth*.

11. Freire, *Educacao*, 40ff.

12. S. Carmichael and C. V. Hamilton, *Black Power* (New York: Vintage Books, 1967), 3, 5, 6.

13. L. Killian and C. Grigg, *Racial Crisis in America* (Englewood Cliffs, N.J.: Prentice-Hall, 1964), quoted in Carmichael, *Black Power*, 55.

14. *Ibid.*, 53.

15. "Les Noirs ont reconnu les sens de la tragedie qu'ils vivent en notre siècle. Ils refusent d'être intégrés à la civilization blanche, car ils la considèrent comme finie. Ils veulent jouer un rôle créateur dans l'histoire. Les écrivains noirs nous avertissent que la civilisation blanche est en train de périr de la servitude qu'elle a imposée aux Noirs." Jan Czernecky, "Révolution Noire aux États Unis," in *Christianisme Social* (Janvier-Fevrier, 1967), 91.

16. Lipset and Wolin, *Berkeley Student Revolt*, 225.

17. *Ibid.*, 219.

18. Freire, *Educacao*, 54, 55.

19. Lipset and Wolin, *Berkeley Student Revolt*, 218.

20. A. V. Pinto, *Consciencia e Realidade Nacional* (Rio de Janeiro: ISEB, 1962), 527.

21. H. Marcuse, *The One-Dimensional Man* (Boston: Beacon Press, 1964), 252.

22. Freire, *Educacao*, 28.

23. *Populorum Progressio* (Boston, St. Paul ed., 1967), no. 34. "The reshaping of society in a more just way, equitable and human, affects more intensely then anybody else, the poor, the workers, the peasants, the social classes which find themselves forcibly maintained on the margin of society, without the possibilities of enjoying properly its goods and services and unable to participate in its decisions; decisions which, exactly because they affect more directly the interests of the poor and outcasts, should not be taken without their active presence. Nobody should take their place in making the basic decisions which concern their own interests, even on the excuse of doing better than themselves." Pedro Arrupe, General Superior of the Jesuits, *Acta Romana Societatis Jesus*, Vol. xiv, fasc. vi (1966), 292–973.

24. Marcuse, *One-Dimensional Man*, 142.

25. Pinto, *Consciencia*, 527.

26. This paraphrase of the biblical text (Mt 6:33) is attributed to Nkrumah. Bola Ige, a representative of an African nation to the World Confer-

ence of Church and Society (Geneva, 1966), comments that "however sacrilegious this might sound to the ears of some people, it does fire the imagination of peoples in the new nations. For us, politics is the most important weapon with which to create a new type of man and society, the new and appropriate systems we want, and to build the strength needed to contend with the older powers." Cf. the Addendum to his address "The Political Dynamics of the New Awakened Peoples," a mimeographed paper, World Conference of Church and Society, Geneva, 1966; conference address no. 9a.

27. I am indebted to Prof. Paul Lehmann for the expression "humanistic messianism," which applies perfectly well to our description of political humanism. *Ideology and Incarnation* (Geneva: John Knox Press, 1962), 25.

28. Quoted in Lewis Mumford, *The Condition of Man* (New York: Harcourt Brace & Co., 1944), 305–306.

29. Henry Clark, "Value Questions and Policy Proposals for a Society of Abundance," *Union Seminary Quarterly Review* 21 (1966), 403.

30. Harvey Cox, *The Secular City* (New York: Macmillan Co., 1965), 184.

31. *Ibid.*, 184.

32. *Ibid.*, 188.

33. Clark, "Value Questions," 403.

34. Cox, *Secular City,* 187–188.

35. Erich Fromm, "The Psychological Aspects of the Guaranteed Income," in *Guaranteed Income: Next Step in Economic Revolution,* ed. Robert Theobald (Garden City, N.Y.: Doubleday & Co., 1966), 176–177.

36. A.Th. van Leeuwen, *Christianity in World History* (London: Edinburgh House Press, 1965).

37. *Ibid.*, 401.

38. *Ibid.*, 403.

39. *Ibid.*, 402.

40. *Ibid.*, 401–402.

41. Marcuse, *One-Dimensional Man,* 12.

42. *Ibid.*, 9.

43. *Ibid.*, 2.

44. *Ibid.*, 33.

45. *Ibid.*, 52.

46. *Ibid.*, xiv.

47. *Ibid.*, xvi.

48. *Ibid.*, xvi.

49. *Ibid.*, x, xii.

50. In one of his theses on Feuerbach, Marx attacked materialism exactly because of this fact: it makes no room for the man who creates the material facts. "The materialist doctrine that men are products of circumstances and upbringing, and, therefore, changed men are products of other circumstances and changed upbringing, forgets that it is men that change circumstances." K. Marx, "Theses of Feuerbach," in *On Religion* (New York: Schocken Books, 1964), 70.

51. John A. T. Robinson, *Honest to God* (Philadelphia: Westminster Press, 1963), 13.

52. D. Bonhoeffer, *Letters and Papers from Prison* (New York: Macmillan Co., 1965), 191.

53. In an article entitled "Reflections after Reading Two Articles on Contemporary Atheism," E. G. Baldo indicates that the option for atheism among students in his country "springs basically from a political choice favoring a social change based on the demand for justice." Cf. *CIF Reports,* Vol. V, p. 27.

54. F. Nietzsche, "Thus Spoke Zarathustra," in *The Portable Nietzsche,* ed. W. Kaufmann (New York: Viking Press, 1965), 127.

55. F. Nietzsche, "The Gay Science," *Portable Nietzsche,* 448.

56. *Ibid.,* 204.

57. *Ibid.,* 452.

58. *Ibid.,* 490. This inhuman character of the language of the Church is not simply the creation of a sick man. In Bonhoeffer we find a similar key being struck. He accuses the Church because in order to be heard she has used a language that makes man unsure about himself, that destroys his emancipation from tutelage and for the world. Apologetics opens its way to man by driving man to despair about life. See his *Letters and Papers from Prison,* 195–196.

59. L. Feuerbach, *The Essence of Christianity* (New York: Harper and Row, 1957), 73, 196.

60. K. Marx, "Contribution to the Critique of Hegel's Philosophy of Right," in *On Religion,* 44–45.

61. Kaufmann, ed., *Portable Nietzsche,* 198.

62. *Ibid.,* 324, 156.

63. *Ibid.,* 282.

64. Cf. Marx, "Contribution to Critique of Hegel," 42.

65. Kaufmann, ed., *Portable Nietzsche,* 188.

66. *Ibid.,* 189.

67. Marx, "Contribution to Critique of Hegel," 42.

68. "What makes us atheists," says Garaudy, "is not our sufficiency, our satisfaction with ourselves and with the earth, with some sort of limitation on our project. The reason is that we, from our experience, similar to the Christian's, of the inadequacy of all relative and partial being, do not conclude to a presence, that of the 'one necessary,' which answers our anguish and impatience. If we reject the very name of God, it is because the name implies a presence, a reality, whereas it is only an exigency which we live, a never satisfied exigency of totality and absoluteness, of omnipotence as to nature and of perfect loving reciprocity of consciousness. We can live this exigency and we can act out of it, but we cannot conceive it, name it or expect it. . . . we must assume the risk every step of the way, since for us atheists nothing is promised and no one is awaiting." Roger Garaudy, *From Anathema to Dialogue* (New York: Herder and Herder, 1966), 65, 94.

69. M. Heidegger, *Being and Time* (New York: Harper & Row, 1962), 220.

70. S. Kierkegaard, *Concluding Unscientific Postscript* (Princeton, N.J.: Princeton University Press, 1941), 75.

71. *Ibid.*, 188.

72. *Ibid.*, 186.

73. *Ibid.*, 218.

74. R. Bultmann, *Kerygma and Myth* (New York: Harper & Row, 1961), 3.

75. *Ibid.*, 15.

76. *Ibid.*, 198, 211.

77. S. Kierkegaard, *Sickness unto Death* (Garden City, N.Y.: Doubleday & Co., Anchor Books, 1954), 146, 162–163.

78. Heidegger, *Being and Time*, 310. "Being-towards-death is essentially anxiety."

79. Kierkegaard, *Concluding Unscientific Postscript*, 32, 112.

80. Heidegger, *Being and Time*, 174.

81. Kierkegaard, *Concluding Unscientific Postscript*, 306.

82. Bultmann, *Kerygma and Myth*, 315.

83. Kierkegaard, *Concluding Unscientific Postscript*, 189. "If one who lives in the midst of Christendom goes up to the house of God, the house of the true God, with the true conception of God in his knowledge, and prays, but prays in a false spirit; and one who lives in an idolatrous community prays with the entire passion of the infinite, although his eyes rest upon the image of an idol: where is there most truth? The one prays in truth to God though he worships an idol; the other prays falsely to the true God, and hence worships in fact an idol."

84. *Ibid.*, 181.

85. Ibid., 73. "The entire essential content of subjective thought is essentially secret, because it cannot be directly communicated."

86. Bultmann, *Kerygma and Myth*, 25–26.

87. *Ibid.*, 319–320.

88. *Ibid.*, 19.

89. *Ibid.*, 19.

90. I. Kant, *What is Enlightenment?* and *Foundations of the Metaphysics of Morals*, tr. Lewis W. Beck (New York: Bobbs-Merrill Co., The Library of Liberal Art, 1959), 85.

91. Cf. K. Barth, *The Word of God and the Word of Man* (New York: Harper & Row, 1957).

92. K. Barth, *The Epistle to the Romans* (6th ed. London: Oxford University Press, 1933), 425.

93. K. Barth, *Church Dogmatics CD* I/2, 50.

94. *CD* I/2, 58.

95. *CD* II/1, 76.

96. *CD* I/2, 63.

97. *CD* II/1, 190.

98. *Ibid.*, 187.

99. Charles C. West, *Communism and the Theologians* (New York: Macmillan Co., 1958), 179.

100. Barth, *Epistle to the Romans*, 91.

101. *Ibid.*, 77.

102. West, *Communism*, 180, quoting *Der Romerbrief*, 2d ed.

103. *CD* I/2, 111.

104. *Ibid.*, 61: "God reveals himself—this is said in view of the factual resistance of man to the divine Lordship. . . . The old aeon is rather God's time confronting men who boast of their own power and in that very fact are sinful and fallen."

Ibid., 67–68. "The fulfillment of time by revelation does not so far mean, of course, the completion, but it means only the announcement, the immediate imminence of the taking away of our time. . . . So far as revelation is not yet redemption but (Mk 1:15) only the 'at handness' of the Kingdom of God itself, our time is actually conserved."

105. Barth, *Epistle to the Romans*, 478.

106. *CD* I/2, 67.

107. Barth, *Epistle to the Romans*, 90.

108. *Ibid.*, 77.

109. *CD* II/1, 468.

110. West, *Communism*, 269.

111. K. Barth, "The Humanity of God," in *God, Grace and Gospel* (Scottish Journal of Theology Occasional Papers No. 8, Edinburgh, London: Oliver & Boyd, 1959), 35.

112. *CD* I/1, 153.

113. *CD* I/2, 45, 50.

114. *CD* I/1, 164: "An act is . . . a relative alternation in the environment which proceeds from it.

CD II/1, 53: Revelation, as the act whereby God makes himself known, means "the giving of signs," "means sacrament . . . in the form of creaturely objectivity."

115. *CD* II/2, 94.

116. *CD* II/2, 177.

117. G. C. Berkouwer, *The Triumph of Grace in the Theology of Karl Barth* (Grand Rapids, Michigan: Wm. B. Eerdmans Publishing Co., 1956).

118. *CD* I/2, 8.

119. *Ibid.*, 52, 51, 58.
120. *CD* I/1, 165.
121. *CD* I/2, 109.
122. *Ibid.*, 82.
123. *Ibid.*, 89.
124. *Ibid.*, 101.
125. *Ibid.*, 110.
126. *Ibid.*, 114.
127. *Ibid.*, 114.
128. *Ibid.*, 56.
129. *Ibid.*, 107.
130. *CD* III/2, 490.
131. *CD* IV/3, 326.
132. *CD* III/2, 526.
133. *Ibid.*, 116.
134. *Ibid.*, 70.
135. *Ibid.*, 66.
136. *Ibid.*, 66.
137. *CD* I/1, 170.
138. *CD* III/4, 520.
139. *Ibid.*, 553.
140. Jurgen Moltmann, *Theology of Hope* (London: SCM Press, 1965).
141. *Ibid.*, 86.
142. *Ibid.*, 84.
143. *Ibid.*, 86.
144. *Ibid.*, 16.
145. *Ibid.*, 43.
146. *Ibid.*, 16.
147. *Ibid.*, 99.
148. *Ibid.*, 16.
149. *Ibid.*, 103.
150. *Ibid.*, 103.
151. *Ibid.*, 85.
152. *Ibid.*, 194.
153. *Ibid.*, 194.
154. *Ibid.*, 88.
155. *Ibid.*, 17.
156. *Ibid.*, 107.
157. *Ibid.*, 112. "Between promise and fulfillment stretches the process of history of the working of the word."
158. *Ibid.*, 103, 102.
159. *Ibid.*, 88.
160. *Ibid.*, 16.
161. *Ibid.*, 18.

162. *Ibid.*, 180.
163. *Ibid.*, 164.
164. *Ibid.*, 104.
165. *Ibid.*, 18.
166. *Ibid.*, 19.
167. *Ibid.*, 210.
168. *Ibid.*, 209.
169. *Ibid.*, 103.
170. Pinto, *Consciencia e Realidade Nacional*, 527.
171. Marcuse, *One-Dimensional Man*, 257, quoting Walter Benjamin, "Nur um der Hoffungslosen willen ist uns die Hoffnung gegeben."
172. Moltmann, *Theology of Hope*, 164.
173. *Ibid.*, 196.
174. *Ibid.*, 25.
175. *Ibid.*, 25.
176. *Ibid.*, 288–289.
177. *Ibid.*, 335.
178. *Ibid.*, 22.
179. *Ibid.*, 22.
180. *Ibid.*, 89.

181. It could be objected that since profane and secular are synonymous, the expression "profanization of the secular" is a tautology. I am reserving the use of the word "profane" not only to designate a world that has emancipated itself from the temple (*profanus*: *pro*, before; *fanum*, a temple) but which, because of this same fact, *is considered as having been made poorer*. This is the world which is void of transcendence, the world of causality of the Kantian philosophy, the world of objective structures of existentialism. To this "profane" world, a sphere of transcendence is opposed, the world of freedom, of the categorical imperative (Kant), the sphere of the "existential" (existentialism). The word "secular," on the contrary, will convey rejection of the deflation of the world, implied in the "profane." It will reject the singling out of a non-worldly sphere for the transcendent. It indicates rather that the secular is precisely the expression of transcendence and that therefore the opposition between sacred and profane, world and transcendence, is brought to an end. Cf. Chapter Six, "Theology As a Language of Freedom."

182. We find a similar proposal in Barth, *Community, State and Church* (New York: Doubleday & Co., 1960), 169. He suggests that the state must be considered an allegory of the Kingdom of God which the Word speaks about. Therefore the state is to be shaped in accordance with this allegorical or analogical relation. The Platonic way of thinking is too obvious to require discussion. The problem with this type of proposal, which was embodied in the idea of the "responsible society," is that it is not borne out of the negation of a definite historical present. Consequently this vision

remains as a dogmatic idea, unable to be mediated into history.

183. Ebeling, *Nature of Faith*, 188.

184. *Ibid.*, 188.

185. *Ibid.*, 187.

186. *Ibid.*, 21.

187. *Ibid.*, 27. For further discussion of this theme see p. 87ff: "An historical language."

188. Barth, *Epistle to the Romans*, 425. Lehmann, *Ethics in a Christian Context*, 74.

NOTES TO CHAPTER TWO

1. Lehmann, *Ideology and Incarnation* (Geneva: John Knox Press, 1962), 25.

2. G. E. Wright, *God Who Acts* (London: SCM Press, 1960), 43.

3. M. Buber, *The Prophetic Faith* (New York: Harper & Row, 1960), 71.

4. *Ibid.*, 72.

5. A. Th. van Leeuwen, *Christianity in World History* (London: Edinburgh House, 1965), 55.

6. Wright, *God Who Acts*, 39.

7. G. E. Wright, *The Old Testament against Its Environment* (London: SCM Press, 1960), 44–45.

8. Van Leeuwen, *Christianity in World History*, 158.

9. *Ibid.*, 77.

10. *Ibid.*, 78.

11. *Ibid.*, 331.

12. See Rom 8:15, 3:27; Gal 5:1; 2 Cor 3:7–9.

13. Mark 2:27.

14. R. Bultmann, *Theology of the New Testament* (New York: Charles Scribner's Sons, 1955), 260.

15. J. Moltmann *Theology of Hope* (London: SCM Press, 1965), 29.

16. Bultmann, *Theology of the New Testament*, 315, 322, 335.

NOTES TO CHAPTER THREE

1. P. Lehmann, *Ideology and Incarnation* (Geneva: John Knox Press, 1962), 25.

2. *Ibid.,* 25.

3. K. Marx, "Preface to a Contribution to the Karl Marx Critique of Political Economy," in Erich Fromm, *Marx's Concept of Man* (New York: Frederick Ungar, 1961), 218.

4. H. Marcuse, *One-Dimensional Man* (Boston: Beacon Press, 1964), 257.

5. Lehmann, *Ideology and Incarnation,* 26.

6. G. E. Wright indicates that this was the central experience of the people of Israel. "Israel as an oppressed minority group in Egypt was marvelously delivered, led through a bleak, inhospitable wilderness, and given a land in which to dwell. . . . The Exodus or deliverance from Egypt, therefore, is the central or focal point in Israelite history and faith." *The Old Testament against Its Environment* (London: SCM Press, 1960), 49–50.

7. N. J. Snaith, *The Distinctive Ideas of the Old Testament* (London: Epworth Press, 1944), 48.

8. Gerhard Von Rad, *Old Testament Theology* (New York: Harper & Row, 1967), I:121.

9. G. E. Wright, *God Who Acts* (London: SCM Press, 1960), 55.

10. See Deut 6:20–24; Joshua 24.

11. Von Rad, *Old Testament Theology,* I:121. G. E. Wright strongly supports this view of the historical character of the language of the biblical communities of faith. "Biblical theology," he remarks, "is first and foremost a theology of recital, in which Biblical man confesses his faith by reciting the formative events of his history as the redemptive handiwork of God." *God Who Acts,* 38.

12. Von Rad, *Old Testament Theology,* I:116.

13. "From first to last Israel manifestly takes as her starting-point the absolute priority in theology of event over *logos." Ibid.,* 116.

14. *Ibid.,* 117.

15. Wright, *God Who Acts,* 44.

16. Lehmann, *Ideology and Incarnation,* 26: ". . . *messianic humanism* . . . subordinates every interpretation of the incarnation to the messianic criterion."

17. K. Barth, *Church Dogmatics* I/2, 137.

18. Paul Minear, *Eyes of Faith* (Philadelphia: Westminster Press, 1946), 221.

19. "Time is an expression of spirit; its momentum marks the pressure of spirit seeking its goal." *Ibid.,* 108.

20. *Ibid.,* 227.

21. Albert Schweitzer, *The Quest of the Historical Jesus* (New York: Macmillan Co., 1964). Cf. Chapter XIX, "Throughgoing Scepticism and Throughgoing Eschatology," 330ff.

22. *Ibid.,* 359.

23. *Ibid.,* 353: "His life at this period was dominated by a 'dogmatic idea' which rendered Him indifferent to all else."

24. Minear, *Eyes of Faith,* 16.

25. Moltmann's understanding of the relation between pregnancy and hope is just the opposite. It is hope that creates the pregnancy, it is the vision of the future that makes man move.

26. M. Buber, *The Prophetic Faith* (New York: Harper & Row, 1960), 142.

27. K. Barth, "The Humanity of God," in *God, Grace and Gospel* (Edinburgh, London: Oliver and Boyd, 1959).

28. Barth, *CD* II/2, 94, 120.

NOTES TO CHAPTER FOUR

1. J. Moltmann, *Theology of Hope* (London: SCM Press, 1965), 25.

2. F. Nietzsche, *Thus Spoke Zarathustra,* in *Portable Nietzsche,* ed. W. Kaufmann (New York: Viking Press, 1965), 137.

3. *Ibid.,* 139.

4. The biblical anthropology, therefore, like its theological language, is derived from acts in history. The answer to the question "what is man?" is not provided by an analysis of man's being as a closed entity, but rather from what man does in history. Anthropology, therefore, is the language that describes man's historicity, namely, what he does in history.

5. Jer 2:2, 20, 21, 24; Hosea 9:1, 11:1.

6. It seems to me that myth, in the context of the radically historical experience of the community of faith, is to be understood as a symbolic generalization of the historical experience. It is an attempt to express and to interpret what was given in history. It is, therefore, a historical way of thinking that has as much validity as the procedures of generalization that have dominated the Western way of thinking.

7. R. Bultmann, *Kerygma and Myth* (New York: Harper & Row, 1961), 242.

8. "That is why," R. Niebuhr observes, "Christian orthodoxy has

consistently defined unbelief as the root of sin, or as the sin which precedes pride. Martin Luther, in conformity with the general Christian tradition and quoting Sirach 10:14, writes in his *Treatise on Christian Liberty*: 'The wise man has said: The beginning of all sin is to depart from God and not trust Him.' " Reinhold Niebuhr, *The Nature and Destiny of Man* (New York: Charles Scribner's Sons, 1949), 183.

9. This process expressed itself in the history of the biblical communities in many different ways. On the one hand, the ark, once the symbol of the dynamic and future-looking God, came to a halt in the temple. Buber observes that in this "polar relation of the ark (the movable) and the temple (the stationary) conceptions we meet the classic expression of the tensions between the free God of history and the fettered deity of natural things." M. Buber, *Prophetic Faith* (New York: Harper & Row, 1960), 83. It seems that the same process was involved in the change of Israel's political institutions. The people's demand to have a king (I Sam 8:5, 20) sounded to the prophet like the rejection of the Exodus experience as the normative for their settled life and as an option for the ways of the "nations," that is, the ways of nature (cf. 1 Sam 8:7–8). The king would mean the end of the open character of their society, which would then become dominated by "organization" and by the requirements of defense (8:11–18). Law and liturgy underwent a similar metamorphosis. If law was a sort of discipline on the way toward the future, liturgy was intended to force Israel to relive the historical events which had made them free. Both law and liturgy, however, became frozen and came to function for Israel as ritual did for primitive societies, that is, as the set of rules and actions which are to be obeyed or performed in order to preserve society free from the new and unexpected.

10. Reinhold Niebuhr, *Moral Man and Immoral Society* (New York: Charles Scribner's Sons, 1932).

11. This is a paraphrase of Reuben Clark's justification of the principles of the Monroe Doctrine. See R. A. Goldwin, ed., *Readings in American Foreign Policy* (New York: Oxford University Press, 1959), 193.

12. Niebuhr, *Moral Man and Immoral Society*, 117.

13. "Justice being taken away, then, what are the kingdoms but great robberies? For what are robberies themselves, but little kingdoms? The band itself is made up of men; it is ruled by the authority of a prince, it is knit together by the pact of the confederacy; the booty is divided by the law agreed on. If, by the admittance of abandoned men, this evil increases in such a degree that it holds places, fixes abodes, takes possessions of cities, and subdues peoples, it assumes the more plainly the name of a kingdom, because the reality is now manifestly conferred on it, not by the removal of coveteousness, but by the addition of impunity." Augustine, *The City of God* (New York: The Modern Library, 1950), IV:4. For the discussion of the relation of justice with the Roman Republic, see XIX:21.

14. Reinhold Niebuhr, *The Nature and Destiny of Man* (New York: Charles Scribner's Sons, 1949), I:212.

15. P. Lehmann, *Ethics in a Christian Context* (New York: Harper & Row, 1963), 97.

16. G. S. Hendry, *The Gospel of the Incarnation* (Philadelphia: Westminster Press, 1958), 142.

17. *Ibid.*, 139.

18. Cullmann suggests that "Jesus, like Barabbas, was condemned by the Romans and not by the Jews, and in fact as a Zealot." See *The State in the New Testament* (New York: Charles Scribner's Sons, 1956), 48.

19. D. Bonhoeffer, *Letters and Papers from Prison* (New York: Macmillan Co., 1965), 219–220.

20. M. Friedmann, *Martin Buber* (Chicago: University of Chicago Press, 1956), 255.

21. Buber, *Prophetic Faith*, 97.

22. M. Buber, quoted in Friedmann, *Martin Buber*, 155.

23. Hendry, *Gospel of the Incarnation*, 140.

24. E. Bloch, *Philosophische Grundfragen* (Frankfurt: Suhrkamp, 1961), I:65.

25. It seems to me that here is one of the reasons why Niebuhr's theology, otherwise so rich in critical resources, has tended to take more conservative positions. His theology sees the cross not primarily as a radical negation that the presence of God in history addresses to the powers that are, in a concrete situation that is to lead to a movement toward the future, but rather as the total relativization of everything in history, which results in the elimination of the sense of direction toward the future. It is true that everything is relative. But if the cross provides not a direction but rather a relativization of all directions, how is it possible to behave in order to bring about a new tomorrow? I am indebted to Prof. Richard Shaull for this remark. He indicates that the problem with Niebuhr's theology is that it concentrates on the anthropological aspect of the problem and does not make room for the messianic thrust of God's activity. For the whole argument, see "Theology and the Transformation of Society" in *Theology Today*, 25 (April, 1968), 23.

26. Moltmann, *Theology of Hope*, 21.

27. See Rom 8:17; 2 Cor 1:5; Gal 6:17; Phil 3:11, 1 Pe 4:13.

28. D. Bonhoeffer, *Letters and Papers*, 223.

29. Quoted by Friedmann, *Martin Buber*, 155.

30. Christian Beker, "Biblical Theology Today" (Inaugural Address, Princeton Theological Seminary, Feb. 21, 1968, mimeographed), 9–10.

31. It seems to me that the idea of reconciliation, as an ontological reality, stands in Protestant theology as a "dogmatic idea," as something not related to history but rather that which overcomes history. The radically historical character of the language of faith, it seems to me, does not

allow us to use the historical event of Jesus Christ as a take-off point in which our language abandons its rapport with history. The ontological reality of reconciliation could easily become a modern version of hegelianism in which the negative in history is transcended in the realm of the divine. How is it possible to speak about reconciliation if the brutal fact of history is the cross?

32. Buber, *Prophetic Faith*, 140. Cf. 211.

NOTES TO CHAPTER FIVE

1. See D. Bonhoeffer, *Letters and Papers from Prison* (New York: Macmillan Co., 1965), 175.

2. Bonhoeffer suggests that "perhaps the importance of polyphony in music lies in the fact that it is a musical reflection of [the] Christological truth, and that it is therefore an essential element in the Christian life." *Ibid.*, 175.

3. Cf. R. Bultmann, *Kerygma and Myth* (New York: Harper & Row, 1961), 348, 335.

4. M. Friedmann, *Martin Buber* (Chicago: University of Chicago Press, 1956), 71.

5. Esdras Borges Costa, "Oportunidades de Humanizacion que Presenta la Situacion Actual in *Hombre, Ideologia y Revolucion en America Latina* (Montevideo: ISAL, 1965), 16.

6. Norman O. Brown, *Life against Death* (New York: Random House, Vintage Books, 1959), 309.

7. H. R. Niebuhr, *The Responsible Self: An Essay in Christian Moral Philosophy* (New York: Harper & Row, 1963), 143.

8. Fromm, *Marx's Concept of Man* (New York: Frederick Ungar Publishing Co., 1961), 98.

9. A. v. Harnack, *What Is Christianity?* (New York: Harper & Row, 1957), 121.

10. Barth, *Church Dogmatics*, III/4, 519–520, 522.

11. Friedmann, *Martin Buber*, 252. "You know always in your heart that you need God more than everything; but do you not know too that God needs you—in the fullness of his eternity needs you?" M. Buber, *I and Thou* (New York: Scribner, 1958), 82.

12. Friedmann, *Martin Buber*, 133, quoting Buber.

13. C. F. Mooney, *Teilhard de Chardin and the Mystery of Christ* (New York: Harper & Row, 1966), 151–152.

14. "The true meaning of the ethical is 'to help God by loving his creation in his creatures. . . .' " Friedmann, *Martin Buber*, 138, quoting Buber.

15. Cf. Marx's "Theses on Feuerback," No. XI, in *On Religion* (New York: Schocken Books, 1964), 72.

16. Thomas Aquinas, *Summa Theologica* (Boston: Benziger Bros. Inc., 1948), I, q.4, a.9.

17. K. Marx, "Alienated Labor," in Fromm, *Marx's Concept of Man*, 101.

18. Cf. L. Feuerbach, *The Essence of Christianity* (New York: Harper & Row, 1957), xxxiv.

19. *Ibid.*, 91.

20. *Ibid.*, 82–83.

21. R. Bultmann, *Kerygma and Myth* (New York: Harper & Row, 1961), 335.

22. Cf. William Temple, *Nature, Man and God* (London: Macmillan & Co., 1964), 478.

23. M. Luther, "That These Words *'This is My Body, etc.,'* "in *Luther's Works* (St. Louis: Concordia Publishing House), 37: 57–58.

24. Cf. John Baillie, *Our Knowledge of God* (New York: Charles Scribner's Sons, 1959), 189ff. Philip S. Watson, *Let God Be God* (Philadelphia: Fortress Press, 1947), 80, 104, 113.

25. Teilhard de Chardin, *The Divine Milieu* (New York: Harper & Row, 1960), 66, 89, 108–109.

26. Song "Como Dois e Dois Sao Quatro" (Denoy de Oliveira e Ferreira Gular): "Como dois e dois sao quatro sei que a vida vale a pena, embora o pao seja pouco e a liberdade pequena. Como teus olhos sao claros e a tua pele morena, como e azul o oceano e a lagoa serena, como um tempo de alegria por tras do terror me acena, e a noite carrega o dia no seu seio de acucena, como dois e dois sao quatro sei que a vida vale a pena."

27. Bonhoeffer, *Letters and Papers*, 103.

28. Feuerbach, *Essence of Christianity*, 278.

29. F. Nietzsche, "Towards a Genealogy of Morals," *Portable Nietzsche*, ed. W. Kaufmann (New York: Viking Press, 1965), 452.

30. Quoted in Fromm, *Marx's Concept of Man*, 132, 144.

31. Brown, *Life Against Death*, 307, 317.

NOTES TO CHAPTER SIX

1. L. Feuerbach, *Essence of Christianity* (New York: Harper & Row, 1957), xxxiv.

2. D. Bonhoeffer, *Letters and Papers from Prison* (New York: Macmillan Co., 1965), 190.

3. S. Freud, *The Future of an Illusion* (Garden City, N.Y.: Doubleday & Co., 1961), 47–49, 69–71.

4. G. E. Wright, *God Who Acts* (London: SCM Press, 1960), 83.

5. *Ibid.*, 107.

6. P. Minear, *Eyes of Faith* (Philadelphia: Westminster Press, 1946), 216.

7. Quoted in Minear, *Eyes of Faith*, 60, from R. Kroner, *How Do We Know God?* (Harper, 1943), 111.

8. "In the Hebrew and Christian view of history the past is a promise to the future; consequently, the interpretation of the past becomes a prophecy in reverse." K. Löwith, *Meaning in History* (Chicago: University of Chicago Press, 1964), 6.

9. F. Kaufmann, *Philosophy and Phenomenological Research* 4 (March, 1944), 296.

10. Quoted by Minear, *Eyes of Faith*, 203.

11. L. Kolakowski, "The Priest and the Jester," in Maria Kuncewicz, ed., *The Modern Polish Mind* (New York: Grosset & Dunlap, 1963), 306.

12. *Ibid.*, 325.

13. *Ibid.*, 326.

14. *Ibid.*, 326.

15. Thomas S. Kuhn, *The Structure of Scientific Revolutions* (Chicago: The University of Chicago Press, 1966).

BIBLIOGRAPHY

Aquinas, Thomas. *Summa Theologica.* Translated by the Fathers of the English Dominican Province. Cincinnati, Chicago, San Francisco: Benziger Bros., 1948.

Aristotle. *Metaphysics.* Translated by Richard Hope. Ann Arbor: The University of Michigan Press, Ann Arbor Books, 1963.

————. *The Nicomachean Ethics.* Baltimore: Penguin Books, 1965.

Augustine. *The City of God.* Translated by Marcus Dods. New York: The Modern Library, 1950.

Baillie, John. *Our Knowledge of God.* New York: Charles Scribner's Sons, 1959.

Barth, Karl. *Church Dogmatics: The Doctrine of the Word of God,* I/1. Edinburgh: T. & T. Clark, 1936.

————. *Church Dogmatics: The Doctrine of the Word of God,* I/2. Edinburgh: T. & T. Clark, 1956.

————. *Church Dogmatics: The Doctrine of God,* II/1. New York: Charles Scribner's Sons, 1957.

————. *Church Dogmatics: The Doctrine of God,* II/2. Edinburgh: T. & T. Clark, 1957.

————. *Church Dogmatics: The Doctrine of Creation,* III/2. Edinburgh: T. & T. Clark, 1960.

————. *Church Dogmatics: The Doctrine of Creation,* III/4. Edinburgh: T. & T. Clark, 1961.

————. *Community, State and Church.* Garden City, N.Y.: Doubleday & Company, 1960.

————. *The Epistle to the Romans.* Translated by Edwyn C. Hoskyns. London: Oxford University Press, 1933.

————. *God, Grace and Gospel.* Scottish Journal of Theology Occasional Papers, N. 8. Edinburgh, London: Oliver & Boyd, 1959.

————. *God in Action.* New York: Round Table Press, Inc., 1936.

————. *The Word of God and the Word of Man.* New York: Harper & Row, 1957.

Berdjaev, N. A. *Slavery and Freedom.* New York: Charles Scribner's Sons, 1944.

Berkouwer, G. C. *The Triumph of Grace in the Theology of Karl Barth.* Grand Rapids, Michigan: Wm. B. Eerdmans Publishing Co., 1956.

Bonhoeffer, Dietrich. *Act and Being.* New York: Harper & Row, 1961.

————. *Ethics.* Translated by Neville Horton Smith. New York: Macmillan Co., 1949.

————. *Letters and Papers from Prison.* Translated by Reginald H. Fuller. Edited by Eberhard Bethge. New York: Macmillan Co., 1965.

Braaten, Carl E. *New Directions in Theology Today.* History and Hermeneutics, vol. 2. Philadelphia: Westminster Press, 1966.

Brown, Norman O. *Life Against Death: The Psychoanalytical Meaning of History.* New York: Random House, Vintage Books, 1959.

Buber, Martin. *I and Thou.* New York: Charles Scribner's Sons, 1958.

————. *The Prophetic Faith.* New York: Harper & Row, 1960.

Bultmann, Rudolf. *History and Eschatology: The Presence of Eternity.* New York: Harper & Row, 1962.

————. *Kerygma and Myth.* New York: Harper & Row, 1961.

————. *Theology of the New Testament.* New York: Charles Scribner's Sons, 1955.

Carmichael, S., and Hamilton, C. *Black Power.* New York: Vintage Books, 1967.

Cochrane, Charles Norris. *Christianity and Classical Culture.* London, New York, Toronto: Oxford University Press, 1957.

Cohen, M., and Hale, D. *The New Student Left.* Boston: Beacon Press, 1966.

Collingwood, R. G. *The Idea of History.* New York: Oxford University Press, 1965.

Cox, Harvey. *The Secular City.* New York: Macmillan Co., 1965.

Cullmann, Oscar. *Christ and Time.* Philadelphia: Westminster Press, 1950.

————. *The State in the New Testament.* New York: Charles Scribner's Sons, 1956.

Dewart, Leslie. *The Future of Belief: Theism in a World Come of Age.* New York: Herder and Herder, 1966.

Ellul, Jacques. *The Presence of the Kingdom.* Translated by Olive Wyon. Philadelphia: Westminster Press, 1951.

————. *Propaganda: The Formation of Man's Attitudes.* New York: Alfred A. Knopf, 1965.

————. *The Technological Society.* New York: Alfred A. Knopf, 1964.

Fanon, Frantz. *The Wretched of the Earth.* Translated by Constance Farrington. New York: Grove Press, 1966.

Feuerbach, Ludwig. *The Essence of Christianity.* Translated by George Eliot. New York: Harper & Row, 1957.

Freire, Paulo. *Educacao como Pratica de Liberdade.* Rio de Janeiro: Editora Civilizacao Brasileira, 1967.

Freud, Sigmund. *The Future of an Illusion.* Garden City, N.Y.: Doubleday & Company, 1964.

Friedman, Maurice S. *Martin Buber: The Life of Dialogue.* Chicago: University of Chicago Press, 1956.

Fromm, Erich. *Marx's Concept of Man.* New York: Frederick Ungar Publishing Co., 1961.

Garaudy, Roger. *From Anathema to Dialogue.* Translated by Luke O'Neil. New York: Herder and Herder, 1966.

Gonzalez, Justo. *Revolucion y Encarnacion.* Puerto Rico: Libreria "La Reforma," 1965.

Harnack, A. v. *What is Christianity?* New York: Harper & Row, 1957.

Heidegger, Martin. *Being and Time.* Translated by John Macquarrie and Edward Robinson. New York: Harper & Row, 1962.

Hendry, G. *The Gospel of the Incarnation.* Philadelphia: Westminster Press, 1958.

Hoekendijk, J. C. *The Church Inside Out.* Philadelphia: Westminster Press, 1964.

Holl, Karl. *The Cultural Significance of the Reformation.* Translated by Karl and Barbara Hertz and John H. Lichtblau. Cleveland and New York: World Publishing Co., Meridian Books, 1962.

ISAL, ed. *Hombre, Ideologia y Revolucion en America Latina.* Montevideo: ISAL, 1965.

Kant, Immanuel. *Critique of Practical Reason.* New York: Bobbs-Merrill Co., 1956.

―――. *Critique of Pure Reason.* Translated by Norman Kemp Smith. New York: The Modern Library, 1958.

―――. *Foundations of the Metaphysics of Morals.* Translated by Lewis White Beck. Indianapolis: Bobbs-Merrill Co., 1959.

―――. *Religion Within the Limits of Reason Alone.* Translated by Theodore M. Greene and Hoyt H. Hudson. New York: Harper & Row, 1960.

―――. *What is Enlightenment?* Indianapolis: Bobbs-Merrill Co., 1959.

Kaufmann, Walter. *The Portable Nietzsche.* New York: Viking Press, 1965.

Kierkegaard, Soren. *Concluding Unscientific Postscript.* Princeton, N.J.: Princeton University Press, 1941.

―――. *Fear and Trembling* and *Sickness unto Death.* Translated by Walter Lowrie. Garden City, N.J.: Doubleday & Company, Anchor Books, 1954.

Kuncewicz, Maria, ed. *The Modern Polish Mind.* New York: Grosset and Dunlap, 1963.

Lehmann, Paul L. *Ethics in a Christian Context.* New York: Harper & Row, 1963.

―――. *Ideology and Incarnation.* Geneva: John Knox Press, 1962.

Lipset, S. M., and Solin, S. S., eds. *The Berkeley Student Revolt: Facts and Interpretations.* Garden City, N.Y.: Doubleday & Company, Anchor Books, 1965.

Lowith, K. *Meaning in History.* Chicago, London: University of Chicago Press, 1964.

Luther, Martin. *An Admonition to Peace: A Reply to the Twelve Articles of the Peasants in Swabia.* Works of Martin Luther, vol. 6. Philadelphia: A. J. Holman, 1915.

―――. *Confession Concerning Christ's Supper.* Luther's Works, vol.

37. St. Louis: Concordia Publishing House, 1961.

———. *That These Words of Christ "This is My Body" still stand firm against the Fanatics.* Luther's Works, vol. 37. St. Louis: Concordia Publishing House, 1961.

———. *A Treatise on Christian Liberty.* Works of Martin Luther, vol. 2. Philadelphia: A. J. Holman, 1915.

Macquarrie, John. *An Existentialist Theology.* New York: Harper & Row, 1965.

Marcuse, Herbert. *One-Dimensional Man.* Boston: Beacon Press, 1964.

———. *Reason and Revolution: Hegel and the Rise of Social Theory.* Boston: Beacon Press, 1966.

Marx, Karl, and Engels, Friedrich. *On Religion.* New York: Schocken Books, 1964.

Mendel, Arthur P., ed. *Essential Works of Marxism.* New York: Bantam Books, 1961.

Metz, Johannes, ed. *Is God Dead?* New York: Paulist Press, 1966.

Minear, Paul Sevier. *Eyes of Faith: A Study in the Biblical Point of View.* Philadelphia: Westminster Press, 1946.

Moltmann, Jürgen. *Theology of Hope.* Translated by James W. Heitch. London: SCM Press Ltd., 1965.

Mooney, Christopher F. *Teilhard de Chardin and the Mystery of Christ.* New York: Harper & Row, 1964.

Mumford, Lewis. *The Condition of Man.* New York: Harcourt, Brace & Co., 1944.

Niebuhr, H. Richard. *The Responsible Self.* New York: Harper & Row, 1963.

Niebuhr, Reinhold. *Resurrection and Historical Reason: A Study in Theological Method.* New York: Charles Scribner's Sons, 1957.

———. *Moral Man and Immoral Society.* New York, London: Charles Scribner's Sons, 1932.

———. *The Nature and Destiny of Man: A Christian Interpretation.* 2 vols. New York: Charles Scribner's Sons, 1949.

Nygren, Anders. *Agape and Eros.* Translated by Philip S. Watson. Philadelphia: Westminster Press, 1953.

Oden, Thomas C. *Radical Obedience: The Ethics of Rudolf Bultmann.*

Philadelphia: Westminster Press, 1964.

Oglesby, C., and Shaull, R. *Containment and Change.* New York: Macmillan Co., 1967.

Pinto, Alvaro Vieira. *Consciencia e Realidade Nacional.* Rio de Janeiro: ISEB, 1960.

Plato. *Great Dialogues.* Edited by Eric H. Warmington and Philip G. Rouse. New York: New American Library, 1956.

Ramsey, Paul. *Basic Christian Ethics.* New York: Charles Scribner's Sons, 1950.

Report from Iron Mountain on the Possibility and Desirability of Peace. Introductory material by L. C. Lewin. New York: Dial Press, 1967.

Ritschl, Albrecht. *The Christian Doctrine of Justification and Reconciliation.* Clifton, N.J.: Reference Book Publishers, Inc., 1966.

Ritschl, Dietrich. *Memory and Hope: An Inquiry Concerning The Presence of Christ.* New York: Macmillan Co., 1967.

Robinson, John A. T. *Honest to God.* Philadelphia: Westminster Press, 1963.

Rose, Stephen, ed. *The Development Apocalypse.* Risk, 1967.

Schleiermacher, Friedrich. *The Christian Faith.* 2 vols. New York: Harper & Row, Harper Torchbooks, 1963.

————. *On Religion.* New York: Harper & Row, 1965.

Schweitzer, Albert. *The Quest of the Historical Jesus.* New York: Macmillan Co., 1964.

Selsam, Howard, and Martel, Harry, eds. *Reader in Marxist Philosophy.* New York: International Publishers, 1963.

Shaull, M. R. *Encounter with Revolution.* New York: Associated Press, 1955.

Snaith, N. J. *The Distinctive Ideas of the Old Testament.* London: Epworth Press, 1944.

Teilhard de Chardin, Pierre. *The Divine Milieu.* New York and London: Harper & Row, 1960.

Temple, William. *Nature, Man and God.* London: Macmillan Co., 1964.

Theobald, Robert, ed. *Guaranteed Income: Next Step in Economic Revolution.* Garden City, N.Y.: Doubleday & Co., 1966.

Tucker, Robert. *Philosophy and Myth in Karl Marx.* New York: Cambridge University Press, 1961.

Van Leeuwen, Arend Th. *Christianity in World History: The Meetings of the Faiths of East & West.* Translated by H. H. Hoskins. London: Edinburgh House Press, 1965.

Von Rad, Gerhard. *Old Testament Theology.* 2 vols. Translated by D. M. G. Stalker. New York: Harper & Row, 1967.

Watson, Philip S. *Let God Be God.* Philadelphia: Fortress Press, 1947.

Weber, Max. *The Protestant Ethic and The Spirit of Capitalism.* New York: Charles Scribner's Sons, 1958.

West, Charles C. *Communism and the Theologians: Study of an Encounter.* New York: Macmillan Co., 1958.

World Council of Churches. *Appell und die Kirchen der Welt: Dokumente der Weltkonferenz fur Kirche und Gesellschaft.* Stuttgart and Berlin: Kreuz-Verlag, 1967.

Wright, G. E. *God Who Acts.* London: SCM Press, 1960.

———. *The Old Testament Against Its Environment.* London: SCM Press, 1960.

Articles and Papers

Baldo, E.G. "Reflections after Reading Two Articles on Contemporary Atheism," in *CIF Reports.* Vol. 4. Cuernavaca, Mexico.

Beker, J. C. "Biblical Theology Today." Inaugural Address, Princeton Theological Seminary, February 21, 1968.

Bola, Ige. "The Political Dynamics of the New Awakened Peoples." Address N. 9a, World Conference on Church and Society, July 12, 1966, Geneva. Mimeographed.

Clark, Henry. "Value Questions and Policy Proposals for a Society of Abundance," in *Union Seminary Quarterly Review* 21 (1966): 401–410.

Costa, Esdras Borges. "Oportunidades de humanizacion que presenta la situacion actual." *Hombre, Ideologia y Revolucion en America Latina.* Montevideo: ISAL, 1965.

Czernecky, J. "La Révolution noire aux Etats Unis." *Christianisme Social,* edited by the Mouvement du Christianisme Social, Paris (Janvier-Février, 1967).

Fulbright, J. W. "The Arrogance of Power." *The Congressional Record.* Vol. 112, no. 81, May 17, 1966.

Furter, Pierre. "Caminhos e Descaminhos de uma Politica da Juventude." In *Paz e Terra,* no. 3. Rio de Janeiro, Editora Civilizacao Brasileira.

Kolakowski, Leszek, "The Priest and the Jester." In *The Modern Polish Mind.* Grosset & Dunlap: New York, 1963.

Lehmann, Paul, "Ética Crista, Ética Marxista." In *Paz e Terra,* no. 1. Rio de Janeiro: Editora Civilizacao Brasileira.

Shaull, Richard. "Berdjaev: Perspectiva Crista da Revolucao Social." In *Paz e Terra,* no. 1. Rio de Janeiro. Editora Civilizacao Brasileira.

Shaull, Richard. "Theology and the Transformation of Society." *Theology Today* 25 (1968).

Smith, Rolland F. "A Theology of Rebellion." *Theology Today* 25 (1968).

INDEX

INDEX